Essays and Conversations on Monetary Policy

José Júlio Senna

INSTITUTO BRASILEIRO DE ECONOMIA

Conversations with

Affonso Celso Pastore
Laurence Ball
Charles Goodhart

Copyright © 2015 Instituto Brasileiro de Economia

Rights on this edition reserved to
EDITORA FGV
Rua Jornalista Orlando Dantas, 37
22231-010 | Rio de Janeiro, RJ | Brazil
Phone: 55 0800-021-7777 | 55 21 21-3799-4427
Fax: 55 21-3799-4430
editora@fgv.br | pedidoseditora@fgv.br
www.fgv.br/editora

Printed in Brazil

All rights reserved. The unauthorized reproduction of this publication, on whole or in part, constitutes a violation to copyright (Law n° 9.610/98).

The views presented in this book are the exclusive responsibility of the authors.

1st edition — 2015

General Coordination: Claudio Roberto Gomes Conceição
Cover and layout: Marcelo Nascimento Utrine
Cover image: shutterstock.com
Impression: Group SmartPrinter

CATALOGUING DATA PREPARED BY
THE LIBRARY MARIO HENRIQUE SIMONSEN/FGV

Senna, José Júlio, 1946-
    Essays and conversations on monetary policy: conversations with Affonso Celso Pastore, Charles Goodhart, Laurence Ball, Paul Volcker / José Júlio Senna. – Rio de Janeiro : Instituto Brasileiro de Economia, 2015.
    144 p.

    In partnership with Editora FGV.
    Includes bibliography.
    ISBN: 978-85-225-1679-7

    1. Monetary policy. 2. Inflation (Finance). 3. Stagnation (Economics). 4. Exchange rates. 5. Economic equilibrium. I. Instituto Brasileiro de Economia. II. Fundação Getulio Vargas. III. Title.

CDD – 332.46

Acknowledgements

This book is a product of my work over the last two years at the Applied Economics group of the Instituto Brasileiro de Economia of the Fundação Getulio Vargas (FGV/IBRE). It comprises four essays and four conversations that I have conducted with distinguished former central bankers and monetary economists. In accomplishing this task I benefitted substantially from the support and help of a considerable number of people, to whom I want to express my gratitude.

To begin with, I wish to thank the continuous support and encouragement provided by Luiz Guilherme Schymura, director of FGV/IBRE. A word of thanks is also due to Armando Castelar, who coordinates the Applied Research group, and with whom I have had the privilege to discuss many issues related to my studies. It is also a privilege to have him as the author of the preface to this book.

In addition to Armando, Regis Bonelli, Fernando Veloso, Fernando de Holanda Barbosa Filho and Fernando Dantas made useful suggestions and important observations on specific aspects of the texts. I extend my thanks to all other members of the Applied Economics Research group who, together with those already mentioned, provide the ideal environment for debates and research which prevails at the Institute. I also thank Marcel Balassiano for his efficient research assistance.

Finally, as to the physical production of the book, I have a great debt with Claudio Conceição. I am grateful to him for his initiatives and enthusiasm in regard to this project, as well as to Marieta de Moraes Ferreira, director of Editora FGV, for her support to this publication.

J.J.S., February 2015

Preface

Hailed as the maestro during his long tenure as chairman of the US Federal Reserve Bank, Alan Greenspan has been severely criticized since he left the Fed for having kept interest rates too low for too long, thus feeding the American house market bubble. During the calm years of the "Great Moderation," it appeared that central bankers had mastered the secret of preserving macroeconomic stability to an extent unimaginable in the past. Few guessed that all this calm would be followed by the turmoil of a protracted crisis marked by great instability and low economic growth, one that has already lasted longer than WWII.

With the financial crisis, unconventional monetary policy became the norm. Quantitative easing programs were adopted in the US, the UK, and, more recently, in Japan and the Euro Zone. Forward guidance, once rare, has been widely adopted. Some central banks have even taken to paying negative interest rates on bank reserves, as we've seen in Denmark and Switzerland.

Much as Greenspan's perceived infallibility may have isolated him from seeing systematic risks, central bankers today are again seen as saviors of the economy (and certainly of financial markets). And their policies, if anything, have brought interest rates even further away from market values than in the maestro's years. With good reason, many analysts fret about the exit strategy from this period of ultra-loose monetary policy and the risk of future crises.

This rich context is the subject of José Júlio Senna's extraordinary book. Senna's passion for studying and analyzing monetary policy helps the reader adventure beyond the headlines to deeper understanding. In this work, Senna synthesizes the most important books and papers, scrutinizes the central banks' communiqués, dissects the press interviews, and relentlessly unpacks all policy measures. As you read along, you will recognize how his unparalleled knowledge of monetary policy allows Senna to both contextualize and critique the finer points of our modern macroeconomic landscapes.

The book has two parts. The first comprises four essays on new developments in monetary policy. The second introduces interviews with experts in the area, including both scholars and practitioners. Both parts provide valuable insights as to where monetary policy is currently headed and what to think about that direction. The book is also valuable reading for a course on monetary policy or contemporary macroeconomics, presenting the key issues in a very didactic way, with lots of historical references.

The first essay focuses on the idea of substituting a nominal GDP path for inflation as the main target of monetary policy. This path would be determined by an estimate of potential GDP growth and a target inflation rate. If actual nominal GDP stayed below that path, as has been the case since the inception of the crisis, monetary policy should remain loose. This broader target would force central bankers to balance the goals of price stability and growth, thus giving them greater room to tolerate high inflation when growth was too low. To some extent, this parallels the framework under which the Fed operates, while also providing a clear benchmark against which to compare the central banks' performance.

Monetary policy experts have historically sympathized with the idea, but have remained skeptical of a central bank that in normal times would consider a high inflation, low growth economy acceptable as long as it followed the projected nominal GDP target path. This asymmetry would make the target less credible once the economy was out of the crisis and probably lead to its demise. But not without first compromising the central bank's commitment to low inflation, thus raising the future cost of monetary policy.

This framework was implicit in the Bank of England's management of monetary policy under Mervin King, who for some time tolerated an inflation rate well above its target. But most everywhere else inflation remained adamantly low and soon the concern shifted to how to bring it up, as is currently the case in Japan and the Euro Zone. The idea, so to speak, died out of lack of usefulness. The debate, while it lasted opened up territory for more dovish, heterodox views on monetary policy to deal with the crisis. As carefully described by Senna, this was the case of forward guidance, which eventually incorporated a flavor of nominal GDP target.

The second essay looks at the main tenets of monetary policy before the crisis and tries to assess which parts of this previous consensus are likely to stay in place and what will probably change. The focus is on policy in normal times, not on exceptional measures warranted by a crisis. The story begins with the end of the fixed exchange rate regime of the Bretton Woods agreement: with the adoption of floating exchange rates, local central banks gained control of the money supply and, thus, monetary policy.

The most common instrument of the more inflation conscious governments of the time (1970s) was to establish a target for the expansion of money supply, a policy later also adopted in the US, under Paul Volker as Fed chairman. Senna covers this period, extracting lessons and demonstrating the gradual movement towards the now much more common inflation-targeting regime, explicitly or implicitly adopted by most developed and emerging countries.

The attractiveness of an inflation-targeting regime was and remains a consensus among pundits. Another consensus, though, has lost some of its appeal: that monetary policy should not worry about financial stability and, in particular, credit-fueled asset-price bubbles, limiting itself to mitigating their negative consequences once they blow up. In particular, the current view is that central banks should coordinate monetary and macro-prudential policy instruments to foster economic and financial stability, on equal footing. But this is easier said than done, shows Senna.

In his third essay, Senna goes deep in time and content to examine a topic that to this day many Brazilians still do not understand or even acknowledge, despite their tragic history in this area: "The Costs of Inflation". In addition to the more traditional focus on the redistributive effects of inflation (generally, but not always, penalizing the poor), he covers a host of other costs: welfare losses, menu costs, price level uncertainty, relative price stability, and the implications of the non-adaptation of the tax system. Indexation, Senna shows, is not a magic solution and has negative long-term consequences, by making people more tolerant to inflation.

Senna's fourth essay deals with one of today's hottest topics: the hypothesis that the world economy may be trapped into a secular stagnation. Senna has been an "enthusiast" (in the intellectual sense) of this hypothesis since it was initially put forward by Larry Summers, and as the essay shows Senna has dedicated a lot time and effort to understand the idea, examine the numbers and make his own judgment of how likely and relevant this hypothesis may be.

This secular stagnation is not a consequence of the financial crisis -- it precedes it by about a decade or so -- and, as the name suggests, should be here when the worst of the crisis is over. Its main relevance for this book is the major challenge that it represents to monetary policy, in the sense that, if actual, it may lead to a situation in which "no attainable interest rate will permit the balancing of saving and investment at full employment".

The first decade of this century was, according to this interpretation, a mild case of secular stagnation, in which ultra-low interest rates were necessary to sustain economic growth and full employment, but at the cost of fostering a financial crisis. More generally, if this hypothesis holds true, so the argument goes, the two goals of monetary policy – macroeconomic and financial stability – will no longer be attainable at the same time.

After such deep dives into monetary policy issues, the reader may feel tempted to skip the four interviews in the book's second part. I strongly advise against this. The interviews provide interesting views on the link between theory and actual policy, from the viewpoint of players who played important roles in different times and places in the area of monetary policy.

These interviews are a must read, not only for those more directly involved with the topic, but also for economists in general. They close the book with the same brilliancy that marks Senna's four essays.

This book will cement José Júlio Senna's reputation as monetary policy scholar. The book is simultaneously history lesson, policy guidebook, and introduction to important figures who shape monetary policy, and will inform the discourse for decades to come. Enjoy.

Armando Castelar Pinheiro

Coordinator of Apllied Economics Research at FGV/IBRE

Contents

Part I Essays		**1**
1	**Nominal GDP targeting**	**3**
	Introduction	3
	Numerical thresholds	4
	The NGDP targeting proposal	10
	Obstacles to implementation	13
	References	16
2	**Monetary policy strategy before and after the crisis**	**19**
	The origins of inflation targeting	20
	The consensus before the crisis	24
	The crisis and the policy responses	28
	The disregarded lessons	34
	The future of central banking	39
	References	46
3	**The costs of inflation**	**49**
	The traditional approach	50
	Welfare losses	52
	Menu costs	54
	Price level uncertainty	55
	Relative price variability	57
	Non-adaptation of the tax system	57
	Are the costs of moderate inflation small?	60
	Inflation and the public opinion	61
	The monetarist's view	63
	Central bankers and price stability	65

The case of Brazil	73
References	76

4 On "secular stagnation" and the equilibrium real interest rate   79

The original idea	79
The revival of the hypothesis	81
A supply-side approach	90
The view from the Fed	92
The behavior of the markets	96
Concluding remarks	97
References	100

Part II Conversations   103

5 Conversation with Affonso Celso Pastore   105

Inflation targeting	105
The neutral rate	106
Monetary policy and the exchange rate	109
Nominal GDP targeting	111

6 Conversation with Laurence Ball   113

Monetary policy and the employment objective	113
The dual mandate	114
Hysteresis in unemployment	115
The idea of a 4.0% inflation target	116

7 Conversation with Charles Goodhart   119

Free banking	119
Inflation and financial stability	121
The funding-for-lending scheme	122
External member of the MPC	123

8 Conversation with Paul Volcker   127

Volcker Rule	127
Household-debt crises	129
Quantitative easing	130
Inflation targeting and the dual mandate	132

Part I

Essays

Nominal GDP targeting
Monetary policy strategy before and after the crisis
The costs of inflation
On "secular stagnation" and the equilibrium real interest rate

1

Nominal GDP targeting

Introduction

It is certainly too soon to talk about regime change regarding the way monetary policy is generally conducted. Yet, in recent years, possibly influenced by the resilience of the Great Recession, a number of economists have begun to challenge the current orthodoxy in this area.

As is widely known, since 1990, a large number of countries, some formally, others without a formal announcement, have adopted an inflation targeting regime, which involves setting an explicit goal for inflation, which then becomes the top priority for monetary policy. Of late, though, some professional economists and, in particular, one acting central banker have criticized this policy framework and suggested that there are better alternatives. Rather than targeting an inflation rate, so goes the idea, the central bank should pursue an announced nominal GDP path. In principle, such a path would combine the potential growth rate of real GDP and the desired long-term inflation rate. If the economy operates with a high level of idle resources, this strategy would imply adopting sufficient monetary stimuli to push the nominal GDP towards the proposed path, within a reasonable non-specified time span. If the lower bound for the nominal interest rate has been reached, the central bank should expand money supply by printing money.

This is a system that has never been tested. And if it is true that its adoption may not be imminent, as remarked above, it is also true that the idea will be widely debated in the foreseeable future. In this respect, it is worth noting that a couple of measures recently undertaken by the

Fed can be viewed as perfectly compatible with the spirit of the proposal. The motivation behind the option for those measures has to do with the slow pace of recovery after economic activity bottomed in mid-2009. And the basic idea is to somehow increase the weight given to unemployment in the central bank's reaction function. We have, then, more than one reason to discuss the subject in this essay. And this is what we do next.

Numerical thresholds

As is widely known, the system in place in the US is not inflation targeting, but the so-called dual regime, according to which the Fed is required to conduct monetary policy so as to obtain the maximum possible employment level and price stability. These are goals established by the US Congress and, in order to have any practical meaning, they need some sort of an interpretation by the policy makers. In any event, the fact of the matter is that, at least in recent times, many people (market analysts, professional economists, politicians, members of the government, etc.) started to view the Fed's policy as tilted towards one of the formal objectives (price stability), in detriment of employment. This view may have gained some strength after January 2012, when the Fomc made explicit (for the first time) what their idea of price stability was. In the words of the press release issued at the end of the meeting held on January 25, "the Committee judges that inflation at the rate of 2 percent [...] is most consistent over the long run with the Federal Reserve's statutory mandate", a statement which was misinterpreted by many as indicative of the adoption of the inflation targeting regime by the Fed. At the occasion, the Fomc opted for not specifying a fixed goal for employment (they gave only a range for the unemployment rate, between 5.2% and 6.0%), based on the reasoning that the maximum level of employment is largely determined by nonmonetary factors, and change over time.

If one looks at the projections of inflation made by Fomc members at some of their formal meetings, from the recent crisis onward, one notices that they rarely go above the 2.0% level. This is probably reflection of the belief of the members of the Committee that the deleveraging process, still ongoing, and the large resource gap under which the American economy has been operating in recent years tend to restrain substantial inflationary pressures. But one cannot rule out the hypothesis that estimates made by the policy makers themselves also reflect their expectations that if inflation rates were to leave the comfort zone, the Committee would take the necessary measures to correct the unbalance. When the subject is unemployment, however, there seems to be no reluctance to project numbers well above what can normally be viewed as equilibrium rates.

Moreover, in more than one occasion, Ben Bernanke made clear that he had no sympathy for raising the "target" for the inflation rate, even on a temporary basis, as had been suggested by a number of economists, adding that there would be no support for such a movement among his colleagues at the Fomc.

However, one can conceive of something hopefully capable of being helpful in speeding up the economic recovery (the major concern in recent times) and which does not involve adopting a higher target for inflation. This has to do with admitting the possibility that, for a while, the rate of price growth may reach levels higher than the famous 2.0%. This is equivalent to saying that the just-mentioned "target" should not be viewed as a ceiling, which is clearly different from formally adopting a higher target.

Within the Fomc, voices in this direction started to appear in the second half of 2011. In fact, in a speech made in September of that year, Charles Evans, president of the Federal Reserve Bank of Chicago, stated that he did not think "a temporary period of inflation above 2.0% [was] something to regard with horror", adding that he did not see "our 2.0% goal as a cap on inflation". (Evans 2011, p. 5).

This line of reasoning was supported by vice chairman Janet Yellen, who would later put it this way: "reducing the deviation of one variable from its objective must at times involve allowing the other variable to move away from its objective. In particular, reducing inflation may sometimes require a monetary tightening that will lead to a temporary rise in unemployment. And a policy that reduces unemployment may, at times, result in inflation that could temporarily rise above its target". (Yellen 2012, pp. 13-14).

The message was clear: the Committee's long term inflation goal (2.0%) should not be viewed as a ceiling for inflation.

Evans, Yellen and others (Kocherlakota, for example, from the Minneapolis Fed, who had also taken part in the debate) maintained this discussion with one specific objective in mind: changing the policy and the essence of the Fed's communications with the public, in particular as regards the directives given as to the future of the policy rate.

The zero lower bound (that is, a band between zero and 25 basis point) was reached in mid-December 2008. In announcing what would end up being the latest change in the policy rate, the Fed decided to indicate that future movements in the fed funds rate would only happen in a somewhat distant point in time. The idea was that, by signaling that it would take a long time for the policy rate to be raised again, the central bank would encourage consumers to spend and business to invest.

Forward guidance of this type is part of a central bank's toolkit, being particularly attractive when the zero bound is reached, though it had already been used under different circumstances. In fact, in the US, Alan Greenspan resorted to such an instrument, in August 2003, when the policy rate had been pushed down to 1.0%. At that time, the signaling took the following form: "the Committee believes that policy accommodation can be maintained for a considerable period". In January 2004, the wording changed into "with inflation quite low and resource use slack, the Committee believes that it can be patient in removing its policy accommodation".

More recently, when the strategy was resumed, the wording was: "the Committee anticipates that weak economic conditions are likely to warrant exceptionally low levels of the federal funds rate for some time" (press release of the Fomc meeting held on December 16, 2008). On March 18 of the following year, the final part of the sentence changed into "for an extended period". In this second phase, the style was basically the same adopted previously, during the Greenspan era.

With the passage of time, however, the Fed decided to be more specific as regards what the policy makers meant by an extended period. In August 2011, the forward guidance incorporated a calendar date. The wording became: "economic conditions – including low rates of resource utilization and a subdued outlook for inflation over the medium run – are likely to warrant exceptionally low levels for the federal funds rate at least through mid-2013". This was later altered to "at least through late 2014" (January 2012) and to "at least through mid-2015" (September 2012).

Evans and Yellen were uncomfortable with this approach because they felt that the message was not sufficiently clear. In Yellen's words, "the Committee might eliminate the calendar date entirely and replace it with guidance on the economic conditions that would need to prevail before liftoff of the federal funds rate might be judged appropriate". She added that this would "enable the public to immediately adjust its expectations concerning the timing of liftoff in response to new information affecting the economic outlook. This market response would serve as a kind of automatic stabilizer for the economy: Information suggesting a weaker outlook would automatically induce market participants to push out the anticipated date of tightening and vice versa". (Yellen 2012, p. 22). Yellen was endorsing a proposal previously made by Evans.

In September 2011, Charles Evans, president of the Federal Reserve Bank of Chicago, suggested the specification of numerical thresholds to describe the conditions that would warrant raising rates. The suggestion became known as the 7/3 proposal. In the proponent's own words, "one way to provide more accommodation [when the zero bound had already been reached] would be to make a simple conditional statement of policy accommodation relative to our dual mandate responsibilities. [...] This conditionality could be conveyed by stating that we would hold the federal funds rate at extraordinarily low levels until the unemployment rate falls substantially, say from its current level of 9.1% to 7.5% or even 7.0%, as long as medium-term inflation stayed below 3.0%". (Evans 2011, p. 10). One year later, Narayana Kocherlakota, president of the Minneapolis Fed, made a similar proposal, with different thresholds, namely 2 ¼ percent for inflation and 5.5 percent for unemployment. (Kocherlakota 2012, p. 4).

In November 2012, Evans modified his own proposal. "I am ready to say that 6.5% looks like a better unemployment marker than the 7.0% rate I had called for earlier". As to inflation, he realized that "the

3.0% threshold makes many people anxious", this being the reason he modified the proposal to include a "modest number like 2.5%", the reference being the total PCE index. (Evans 2012, p. 8).

It seems, then, that, the Fomc was maturing the idea of allowing inflation to run at rates that would make members of the Committee uncomfortable in normal times. An attitude in this direction would be equivalent to giving more weight to the unemployment variable than had been the case until then.

It seems fair to say that, in the academic world, the most distinguished opponent of the language (or policy) originally adopted by the Fed was Michael Woodford. His criticism became widely noticed as a result of the paper he presented at the Jackson Hole Symposium, in late August 2012. At that occasion, the argument was put forward as explained below.

In essence, changes in the policy rate affect the economy through the impact they might have on the rates expected to prevail in the future. In other words, it is the future path of the policy rate that really matters. Monetary policy becomes more efficient if the authorities manage to generate expectations in line with the policy-rate path that is judged to be compatible with achieving the established objective.

Woodford emphasizes that market participants need to understand the authorities' reaction function. In his words, "information about policy intentions is likely to affect the expectations of market participants more than information about the central bank's view of the economic outlook, because the way in which the bank intends to conduct policy is a matter about which the bank obviously knows more than do outsiders". (Woodford 2012, p. 33).

Given the fact that it is the anticipated path of the policy rate that really matters for the economic decisions of consumers and firms, and as long as the authorities are confident that they are capable of effectively influencing the expectations regarding the mentioned path, there seems to be no reason for not trying to exert that influence by means of the of the so-called forward guidance mechanism. The point stressed by Woodford is that the ideal type of signaling should involve a sort of communication in which the policy makers state, as clearly as possible, what they intend to do, rather than giving the impression that they are simply engaged into forecast exercises. After all, market participants can always rely more on their own estimates than on the ones produced by the central bank.

If we examine carefully the language adopted by the Fed until the mid of last year, we cannot avoid the conclusion that the signaling lacked the necessary precision. In fact, what is really conveyed when the central bank says that the economic conditions are likely to warrant exceptionally low levels of the policy rate until a certain date? Should the statement be interpreted as a commitment, or as a simple projection? It is quite hard to tell. What if the conditions change, and the economy's recovery somehow speeds up? Will the policy rate be raised, prior to the specified date?

Woodford's paper rapidly became required reading for specialists in the field, particularly because it seems to have influenced the Fed's policy from that point onward. In fact, the first Fomc meeting after the Jackson Hole seminar was held on September 13 (date of the end-of-meeting statement). At that opportunity, the Committee decided to create a new open-ended program of additional purchases of agency mortgage-backed securities and opted for an important change in language. First, the new program is to be maintained until the conditions in the labor market show substantial improvement. Second, "the Committee expects that a highly accommodative stance of monetary policy will remain appropriate for a considerable time after the economic recovery strengths". For the first time, future changes in the course of monetary policy were being tied to economic outcomes (though vaguely defined), leaving behind the previous policy of announcing fixed amounts of purchases of certain securities over predetermined time spans.

On December 12, the change was more radical. The idea of thresholds originally suggested by Charles Evans (adjusted for his own new numbers) was formally implemented. In the end-of-meeting statement, one reads: "the Committee [...] anticipates that this exceptionally low range for the federal funds rate [between zero and ¼ percent] will be appropriate at least as long as the unemployment rate remains above 6-1/2 percent, inflation between one and two years ahead is projected to be no more than a half percentage point above the Committee's

2 percent longer-run goal, and the longer-term inflation expectations continue to be well anchored".

The NGDP targeting proposal

The criterion of thresholds was favorably praised by Michael Woodford prior to its implementation. "Adoption of such a commitment by the Fomc would be an important improvement upon current communication", he said at the Jackson Hole Symposium. (Woodford 2012, p. 43). But Woodford's real preference was for something more drastic, involving a regime change, in which case there would be a commitment on the part of the Fed to pursue a nominal GDP target path.

In the central banking world, a similar way of thinking was expressed by Mark Carney, governor of the Central Bank of Canada and the governor-designate of the Bank of England. As is widely known, these two countries are early adopters of the inflation targeting regime. According to his view, successful practitioners of this regime may lead market participants to believe that inflation would not be allowed to remain above target, and those beliefs may reduce the effectiveness of monetary stimuli, at the cost of delaying economic recovery. Numerical thresholds somehow tie the hands of the central bank, making policy more effective. But Carney claims that this idea exhausts the options available within the current framework. In his opinion, "adopting a nominal GDP-level target could in many respects be more powerful than employing thresholds under flexible inflation targeting". (Carney 2012, p. 8).

Before getting into some detail as to how a nominal GDP targeting strategy would work, let us add that in October 2011 the idea had been publicly defended by Christina Romer, who headed the Council of Economic Advisers during the first 20 months of the Obama administration. In an article published by The New York Times, under the title "Dear Ben: It's Time for Your Volcker Moment", Romer noticed that, as Fed chairman, Paul Volcker had "dramatically changed how monetary policy was conducted". Bernanke should do something similar, that is, he should "stage a quiet revolution of his own". (Romer 2011).

In the late 1970s, the strategy adopted by the Fed was not working, and the main problem of that time (inflation) remained without a solution. Today, the argument continues, inflation is low, but "unemployment is stuck at a painfully high level". As in 1979, "the methods the Fed has used so far are not solving the problem". (Romer 2011). We need, then, a new policy regime.

But how would the proposal work? The potential growth rate of the American economy is generally considered to be around 2.5% per annum. And since the Fed understands that the famous 2.0% is the long-term desired rate of inflation, the target for nominal GDP growth could be reasonably set at 4.5% per year. In order to define the path we need a starting point, capable of being viewed as a "normal" year. In the graph below, we took 2007 as a reference year. The trend is built by extrapolating forward the nominal GDP observed in that year, at a rate of 4.5% per annum. The same graph shows the observed path of NGDP until 2012 as well as the extrapolation of the historical tendency (since 1990) into the future. As one can see, the American economy operates nowadays at a level which is 10.0% below the trend, as defined above. If the comparison is made with the historical NGDP trend (growth rate estimated around 5.3%), the divergence goes up to 15.0%.

Graph 1
US nominal GDP growth

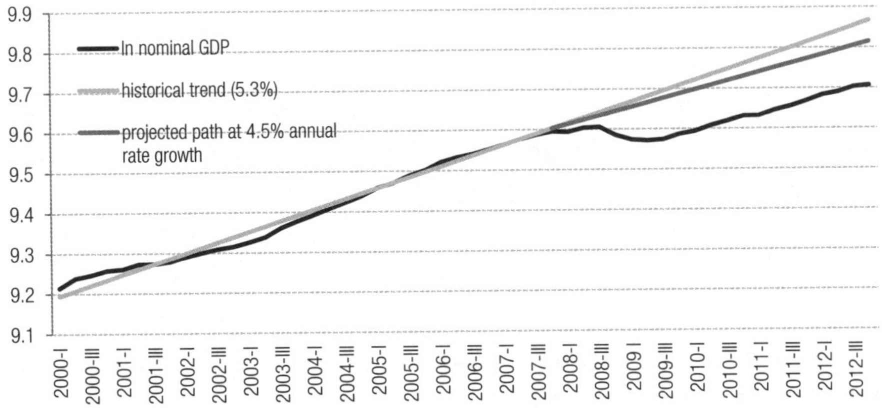

Source: BEA

Adopting the proposal would mean that the Fomc members would be committed to eliminating the gap. Since the Fed does not have enough control of the economy's behavior, it would be advisable not to specify in advance the time span over which the gap will be closed.

In Romer's mind, adopting the mentioned target would be equivalent to the decision taken by Volcker back in 1979, when he announced that the Fed would be targeting the rate of growth of the money supply, defined in a particular way. Supposedly, the main result would also be similar, that is, a considerable improvement in confidence. To the extent that this happened, consumers and firms would increase their spending. The economy would grow faster and the inflation rate might reach higher levels. In this case, a higher inflation rate would be considered helpful, and not a source of concern.

Announcement of the change in the monetary regime would be helpful per se. At least, so goes the argument. But it would surely not be enough to lead the economy to the desired track. This means that the announcement would have to be followed by further monetary actions. In reality, the Fed would need to be prepared to provide additional monetary stimuli, without specifying any limit for that. The so-called quantitative easing would enter into another phase. Still according to the proposal, there would be no reason to worries, since there would be a sort of an exit strategy embodied into the whole program. More specifically, the additional purchases of securities would be interrupted (and the policy rate would be taken to its neutral level) when the target were reached.

A final point needs to be made. How would the central bank evaluate the need for additional monetary actions? The idea here is simple and was already discussed in an old paper on the subject, written by Robert Hall and Gregory Mankiw. As these authors said in the early 1990s, the problem of lags in monetary policy is particularly relevant if a central bank adopts NGDP targeting. In their own words, it takes several months for monetary policy actions to affect the economy, "but the consensus forecast that far in the future is quite responsive to current monetary policy. Within a few days of a change in monetary policy, the consensus forecast changes to reflect expert opinions about the effects on all macro variables, including nominal income". (Hall and Mankiw 1994, p. 78). The solution, then, is to work with forecasts, an idea which would later become a crucial aspect of the modern inflation targeting regime. In fact, in this case, the central banks usually guide their actions by the behavior of the inflationary expectations. As the Swedish economist Lars Svensson once said, "inflation targeting implies inflation forecast targeting: the central bank's inflation forecast becomes an intermediate target". (Svensson 1996, p. 2).

Obstacles to implementation

It is difficult to predict whether the nominal GDP targeting proposal will ever be adopted. The fact is that the idea has been around for more than two decades and so far no one has effectively moved towards its implementation. Would the reason be the fact that the target in this case is harder to be understood by the public than in the case of inflation targeting? Or would it be because conceptually it is generally considered not to be a good strategy?

It may be exact to say that the chances of adopting NGDP targeting are greater now than in the past because the reality is different. More specifically, central banks around the world have made use of a very large set of instruments (conventional and non-conventional ones) with the objective of promoting a rapid economic recovery. Generally speaking, the results have been quite positive, but the truth of the matter is that, so far, a large number of developed economies have not fully recovered from the recent crisis. In addition, the monetary policy strategy that prevailed prior to the crisis has been questioned in several circles. To some extent, it is no surprise that we find people suggesting a regime change, that is, something a bit more radical than what has been tried so far, with the objective of obtaining a more substantial improvement in confidence.

From the middle of this year onward, the Bank of England will be run by someone very sympathetic to the NGDP targeting proposal. Whether Mark Carney's idea will be accepted or not is hard to tell. It very much depends on the Chancellor of the Exchequer. Although a movement in that direction is not presently expected, it is worth noting that surprises happen. In the 1990s, for example, the incumbent chancellor took two surprising measures. Norman Lamont, first, and Gordon Brown, second. Lamont established a target range for the inflation rate (1%-4%) one month after England abandoned her fixed exchange-rate policy. And, five years later, Brown set the Bank of England free to manage the country's interest rate policy.

In the United States, those who defend the new proposal applaud the numerical thresholds policy, already in place. It is possible, then, to look at this latest movement as a preliminary step towards the adoption of the NGDP suggestion. But things are more complicated than that. In the US, the monetary policy's objectives are determined by Congress. And the Fed does not seem to be in a comfortable position to attempt a more radical change. It must be recalled that the much simpler idea of inflation targeting never turned into reality, in spite of the fact that it had a much larger support basis and benefitted from the experience of a quite substantial number of countries.

Besides this, it is not so clear that establishing a target path for nominal GDP is really a good idea. According to the proposal, any combination of inflation and real GDP growth is satisfactory, provided that the final result represents a movement towards closing the gap. If one establishes 4.5% rate of growth per annum for nominal GDP as the desired path, for example, a combination of 4.0% inflation rate and 1.5% real growth would supposedly do it, since this would contribute to diminish the distance to the stipulated path. But the question is: how long would such a scenario prevail? No one can really tell. Inflationary expectations, however, might be hurt, and the price system might lose an important anchor, a reasoning which, to begin with, rules out a large number of countries as potential candidates for the adoption of the NGDP targeting proposal. Economies with a long tradition of high inflation and where inflationary expectations are not well anchored should not even think about that possibility.

Another consideration has to do with the emphasis on economic growth. It took a couple of decades for academics, central bankers and economic analysts in general to understand and accept the fact that there are well-defined limits to what monetary policy can achieve. In the long run, central banks can only affect nominal variables, this being the reason why they should have their attention and efforts geared to the promotion of price stability. Tying their hands and forcing them to pursue economic growth seems quite dangerous, a movement which could put at risk a great deal of the progress so far obtained, particularly as regards the way monetary policy strategies should be conceived.

As is well known, monetary expansion and lower interest rates are demand-management instruments. Depending on the circumstances, aggregate demand may not fully respond to actions taken by policy makers. Marriner Eccles, a former chairman of the board of the Fed (1936-48), was the first to compare monetary policy to a string: while you can pull it to put an end to inflation, you cannot push it to take an economy out of a recession. According to Allan Meltzer, in a testimony before the House Committee on Banking and Currency, in 1935, Eccles' words were; "you cannot push on a string". Apparently, he had in mind a situation later to be known as liquidity trap. (Apud Meltzer 2003, p. 478).

It seems clear that monetary policy did not become totally ineffective, in recent years, as a radical interpretation of this reasoning would imply. In many countries, the economic situation would have gotten a lot worse were it not for the bold measures taken by government authorities, in general, but particularly by the central bankers. But the idea that central banks have been pushing on a string comes to mind when one recalls the enormous amount of monetary stimulus already given, in several countries, and the reluctance of consumers to spend, of banks to lend and of firms to invest. The circumstances, characterized by a long and costly process of deleveraging, made monetary policy much less powerful than in more normal times. Of course, things become even more complicated when a given economy faces severe supply-side bottlenecks, or sees her potential growth rate decline considerably. Monetary policy is unable to provide any sort of compensation for such factors.

As long as problems like these remain relevant, adopting the NGDP targeting proposal might be quite a risky strategy. A point may be reached, for example, in which an enormous amount of stimulus has already been given, with no adequate response on the part of the economy. In other words, forecasts for real GDP and for inflation might show rates of growth of nominal GDP below the established path. According to the new "rules of the game", the central bank would be led to increase purchases of securities, bringing a great deal of discomfort to many people, probably within the central bank in question as well. Inflation expectations may suffer some damage, even in countries in which the monetary authorities have high credibility. In this case, nominal interest rates would incorporate these higher expectations, eliminating (partially or totally) whatever "gains" might have occurred in terms of the lowering of the real interest rates.

But even if inflationary expectations and inflation itself do not go up, and assuming economic growth does not accelerate, the distance to the target might increase, causing the central bank to lose whatever credibility it might have acquired, and perhaps forcing the discontinuation of the program.

In summary, it is not clear that nominal GDP targeting is really a good idea. Based on the reasoning here presented, we do not expect it to be adopted, at least in any reasonable scale. It may become the preferable strategy in one country or another, but it is not likely to get as widespread as the inflation targeting regime did.

References

Carney, Mark, 2012, "Guidance", Bank of Canada, December 11.
Evans, Charles E., 2011, "The Fed's Dual Mandate Responsibilities and Challenges Facing U.S. Monetary Policy", *Federal Reserve Bank of Chicago*, September 7.
---------------, 2012, "Monetary Policy in Challenging Times", *Federal Reserve Bank of Chicago*, November 27.
Federal Reserve Press Release, several issues.
Hall, Robert E. and Mankiw, N. Gregory, 1994, "Nominal Income Targeting", in *Monetary Policy*, ed. By Gregory N. Mankiw, The University of Chicago Press, pp. 71-94.

Kocherlakota, Narayana, 2012, "Planning for the Liftoff", *Federal Reserve Bank of Minneapolis*, September 20.

Meltzer, Allan H., 2003, *A History of the Federal Reserve*, vol. 1, The University of Chicago Press.

Romer, Christina D., 2011, "Dear Ben: It's Time for Your Volcker Moment", *The New York Times*, October 29.

Svensson, Lars E., 1996, "Inflation Forecast Targeting: Implementing and Monitoring Inflation Targets", NBER Working Paper Series, Working Paper 5797, NBER, October.

Woodford, Michael, 2012, "Methods of Policy Accommodation at the Interest-Rate Lower Bound", Jackson Hole Symposium, August 31-September 1.

Yellen, Janet L., 2012, "Revolutions and Evolution in Central Bank Communication", *Board of Governors of the Federal Reserve System*, November 13.

2

Monetary policy strategy before and after the crisis

Frederic Mishkin is a well-known name in the field of monetary economics. In particular, he has written extensively on monetary policy strategies. In a paper presented in the end of last year, he argued that "events in the recent global financial crisis have changed central banking forever". It is hard to disagree with him.

But what is it exactly that requires change, or adaptation? What proved to be flawed in the conduction of monetary policy prior to the recent crisis? What important facts, well known before the recent events, were disregarded by the monetary authorities? To what extent were central banks responsible for the phenomenon known as the Great Recession? What part of the previous strategy, or of the previous consensus, needs to be preserved, and very likely will? An answer to these questions is indispensable if we want to anticipate how monetary policy will be conducted in the future, when the crisis is over. And this is what we intend to do in this essay.

First, we analyze how monetary policy evolved in the years prior to the crisis. In other words, we examine the path it followed until the inflation targeting framework became dominant, at least in spirit. Second, we sum up the main conclusions of the prevailing doctrine shared by both academics and central bankers in the final phase of that period. Third, we briefly describe the recent adverse events and the main lines of the monetary policy responses. Forth, we indicate that a great deal of what many people call "lessons from the crisis" was already known and ended up being ignored for reasons not completely understood. Finally, we discuss what part of the previous consensus will probably be preserved, as well as the most likely directions of the necessary changes. We must stress from the beginning that we leave aside aspects related to monetary policy strategies in times of crisis, although we deal with what to do to minimize the occurrence of such a phenomenon. This means that we shall not deal here with specific proposals advanced with the purpose of accelerating the recovery process.

The origins of inflation targeting

For more than two decades, Milton Friedman led a series of researches aimed at convincing politicians, economists and the public in general that inflation was an important problem and that, contrary to the prevailing theoretical framework, widely known as Keynesianism, monetarism could explain that phenomenon. And it had a solution to offer.

However, as Harry Johnson put it, agreement on the second proposition depended on the acceptance of the first. (Johnson, 1971, p. 7). This only happened in the end of the 1960s and beginning of 1970s, when, in the United States, the rate of price growth reached a significant level. In reality, at that time, inflation became a problem not only for the US but for the world economy in general. At that point, a new theoretical framework had already been built. And two basic monetarists' propositions became widely accepted, namely: a) inflation is a monetary phenomenon; and b) there is a temporary trade-off between inflation and unemployment, but no permanent trade-off.

The acceptance of these ideas had two main implications. First, the fight against inflation should be a task for central banks, which, at least in principle, could control monetary expansion. Second, given the inability of central banks to permanently affect the behavior of real variables, monetary authorities should dedicate themselves to the control of inflation. In some countries, the willingness to do so was present. But they faced a huge problem: the exchange-rate regime in place at that time. In the early 1970s, the world was still under the so-called Bretton Woods system, which implied fixed but adjustable exchange rates. According to this system, individual countries give priority to the foreign price of their currencies. In such cases, attempts to maintain fixed the exchange rates mean absence of control over the domestic money supply.

Germany and Switzerland were the two most relevant examples of countries which entrusted the task of fighting inflation to their central banks, and where priority was given to that task. In those two economies the problem of not having control over the supply of money was particularly severe, since, in the exchange-rate markets, there was a great deal of speculation in favor of their currencies. In other words, the German mark and the Swiss franc were two of the best candidates to appreciate in any realignment of rates or in case the Bretton Woods system broke down. At the same time, the US economy was weakened and experienced substantial deficits in the balance of payments. In a sense, the US was exporting inflation to other countries. To defend their currencies, the Germans and the Swiss were forced to acquire enormous amounts of dollars in the international markets. Capital flows were too huge to be fully sterilized, which implied high rates of monetary expansions. As a consequence, inflation rates were also high. In the early 1970s, in Germany, the rate of price growth varied between 5.0% and 7.0% per year. In Switzerland it was even higher.

With the collapse of the Bretton Woods system in the first months of 1973, the Germans and the Swiss became free to pursue independent monetary policies. The dominant influence of money on prices is something they had already recognized. With the elimination of the constraint imposed by the old exchange-rate regime, they now sensed that their inflation rates could be lower than elsewhere. At the same time, they were convinced of the importance of committing themselves to some sort of a rule in the conduction of monetary policy. And these became the main goals of their central banks.

The strategies adopted in Germany and Switzerland were quite similar. Both countries formally introduced monetary targeting, as they established numerical objectives for the expansion of the money supply. Those parameters were set based on informal targets for the inflation rates and were determined by means of the so-called quantitative equation, considered a valid framework for the medium and long run. The procedure involved hypotheses for the potential rate of economic growth and the trend in the change in velocity. The approach was not a rigid one. In several occasions, the authorities chose to postpone meeting their targets to avoid hurting the pace of economic activity. In fact, very often, monetary targets were not met. In spite of this, the authorities managed to preserve their credibility. In Germany, in particular, the strategy was frequently referred to as "pragmatic monetarism", an expression later to be used in the US, during the Volcker administration.

It is important to stress that very early in the process the authorities of both countries were stimulated to make explicit the hypotheses they were working with as they set up their strategies and numerical targets. In other words, they understood the importance of transparency and good communication. The final results are considered to be quite good. In both economies the average inflation rate converged to less than 2.0% per annum, and stayed at that level for many years.

Several other countries attempted to adopt similar strategies. But they failed. The UK is a case in point. The reasons for such failure and a more detailed analysis of the experience of Germany and Switzerland with monetary targeting can be found elsewhere (Senna, 2010, chapter 12). Here, it suffices to recall some important lessons from the two successful experiences: a) the clear definition of targets for inflation and monetary expansion had a great role to play in coordinating inflationary expectations; b) it imposed discipline on the central banks; c) the strategy helped to contain political pressures on the monetary authorities; d) it gave a basis for evaluating the performance of the central bankers.

In the final years of the 1980s, monetary economics had gone through an important revolution, thanks to the contribution of the so-called new classical economists. Apart from the controversies generated by the new theoretical framework, the fact is that, by that time, economic theory and central bankers in general had already incorporated (apparently in a definitive way) the idea that the effects of monetary policy on the economy depended on expectations regarding the future behavior of the monetary authorities. Besides this, the new way of thinking helped to further clarify the risks involved in monetary activism. In other words, central bankers would operate on safer grounds if they worried basically with the rate of price change, a conclusion already arrived at by the monetarists.

At the same time, on the practical domain, inflation had already been "conquered" in the US. After reaching 14.0% in the late 1970s, it had been brought down to less than 4.0% per annum. A similar phenomenon had also been observed in Europe. In this case, some of the countries which experienced disinflation benefitted substantially from a system known as the exchange-rate mechanism, which implied fixed (but adjustable) exchange rates, centered on the Deutsche mark. The costs of that mechanism proved to be high when, in the early 1990s, the German reunification led the Bundesbank to substantially raise the rate of interest, a policy which was not in the interest of most (if not all) of those which had adhered to that system.

Theoretical support, concrete evidence of success in the fight against inflation and a sense of improved well-being, associated with more modest rates of price growth in several parts of the world, called attention to what in fact works in the field of monetary policy. In particular, a high degree of consensus was formed around the idea that the price system of a given economy works better in the presence of some sort of an anchor.

At the end of 1980s, there had been experiences with two types of anchor: the money supply and the exchange rate. A third one was about to appear, with the introduction of inflation targeting (IT). By making explicit a numerical target for inflation, in this case one goes directly to the final objective. Different countries adopted IT for distinct reasons. The UK and Sweden, for example, had gone through the collapse of the exchange-rate anchor; Canada had experienced frustration with monetary targeting; and New Zealand wished to consolidate gains already obtained in fighting inflation.

Under the new regime, the central bank is given the task to stabilizing the rate of inflation (over the medium term) around the numerical target, which becomes the anchor of the system. The experiences of those which had success with monetary targeting made clear the importance of being flexible. And flexibility became an important characteristic of IT, to the extent that, in conducting their policies, monetary authorities take into consideration the short-term behavior of the real economy. In the presence of shocks, they can postpone the convergence of inflation to the specified target. Inflation can be brought back to the target rather quickly, but that result can be achieved only at the cost of creating excessive output volatility. The new policy regime exhibits what Bernanke and others have called "constrained discretion". (Bernanke et. al., 1999, p. 293).

Another important lesson drawn from the successful monetary targeting experiences was that central banking should not be dealt with (as it used to be) in a mysterious way. In other words, between the then dominant mystique and the transparency of the Germans and the Swiss, IT practitioners opted for the latter. It became clear that considerable benefits can be collected from establishing an objective easily understood by the public and from disclosing the strategies to achieve that objective as well as plans to correct them in case they prove to be mistaken. In democratic societies, transparency and good communication seem to be indispensable mechanisms for monetary authorities to obtain credibility, support from the public and independence to act.

As the IT adopters incorporated the above-mentioned characteristic, they were making monetary policy more predictable, an old proposition made by the monetarists. Milton Friedman, for example, following a tradition initiated by Henry Simons, liked to stress that monetary policy could (and should) be conducted in such a way as to "prevent money from being a major source of economic disturbance". (Friedman, 1968, p. 12).

The consensus before the crisis

In the middle of the years 2000, around 30 countries had become IT practitioners. Both in the academic profession as well as in the world of central banking there was widespread support for flexible inflation targeting. This became the conventional framework, according to which monetary policy should aim at minimizing the variability of inflation around the target and the variability of output (or employment) around the trajectory consistent with low and stable inflation.

The combination of short-term policy flexibility with the discipline imposed by targeting low rates of inflation produced very good results, even in countries where IT had not been formally adopted (the US, for example). Considerable decline in the volatility of output and employment, on the one hand, and of inflation, on the other hand, became a fact of life. Recessions turned into much milder and less frequent phenomena and inflation rates stabilized at quite low levels. We were living through the so-called Great Moderation, a phase generally understood to have lasted from the mid-1980s until the breakdown of the recent crisis.

For those who were conducting monetary policy along the new framework, the basic concerns had to do with meeting the medium-term inflation target, preserving the flexibility to offset cyclical deviations in economic activity and employment, and communicating the chosen plans and strategies. This means that events in the financial markets, however important, were not taken into due consideration.

Thus, during (and prior to) the Great Moderation, monetary and financial stability policies were not integrated. The first one focused only on stabilizing inflation and output, while the second was treated separately. In some circles, at least implicitly, it was admitted that price and output stability would ensure financial stability.

In addition to this sort of dichotomy, one must stress that prudential regulators and supervisors looked at financial stability problems from the micro point of view. In other words, the focus was on the safety and soundness of individual entities. They failed to notice that financial institutions, households and firms can behave in a certain way that, in the aggregate, could lead to unsustainable levels of spending, debt and asset prices.

Discussions on whether or not a central bank should be concerned with the behavior of asset prices, and whether or not it should respond to them, are quite old. It may be exact to say that these issues were brought up by analyses of the circumstances which led to the Great Depression. In fact, writing in the heat of those events, Keynes attributed the primary cause of the problems of that time to the interest-rate policy followed by the Fed, and other central banks as well, wrongly guided by the stock-market boom. In his own words, "the high market-rate of interest which, prior to the collapse, the Federal Reserve System, in their effort to control the enthusiasm of the speculative crowd, caused to be enforced in the United States – and, as a result of sympathetic self-protective action, in the rest of the world – played an essential part in bringing about the rapid collapse. [...]. Thus, I attribute the slump of 1930 primarily to the deterrent effects on investment of the long period of dear money which preceded the stock-market collapse." (Keynes, [1930] 1950, p. 196).

In their book *A Monetary History of the United States*, Friedman and Schwartz were also critical of the Fed's attempt to influence the behavior of the stock market in the period which preceded the crash. They put it this way: "there is no doubt that the desire to curb the stock market boom was the major if not dominating factor in Reserve actions during 1928 and 1929. [...]. In the event, it followed a policy which was too easy to break the speculative boom, yet too tight to promote healthy economic growth". The concluding words were: "the Board should not have made itself an arbiter of security speculation or values and should have paid no direct attention to the stock market boom, any more than it did to the earlier Florida land boom". (Friedman and Schwartz, 1963, pp. 290-292). This view would later be endorsed by several other academic researchers. (See, for example, Hamilton, 1987, pp. 147-154).

In 2002, the year Bernanke became a member of the Fed's Board of Governors, he gave a speech in New York under the title "Asset-Price 'Bubbles' and Monetary Policy". At that occasion, he called attention to the fact that the Fed has two broad sets of responsibilities. One is to promote maximum sustainable employment, stable prices and moderate long-term interest rates. The other is to ensure the stability of the financial system. In his opinion, "the Fed should use monetary policy to target the economy, not the asset markets". And to help ensure financial stability, the Fed should use "its regulatory, supervisory and lender-of-last resort powers." (Bernanke, 2002, p. 2).

Monetary policy should not lean against bubbles for two reasons. First, the central bank "cannot reliably identify bubbles in asset prices. Second, even if it could identify bubbles, monetary policy is far too blunt a tool for effective use against them". (Bernanke, 2002, p. 3). The idea is that attempts to influence the prices of a certain class of assets, by means of monetary policy actions, unavoidably affect the broader economy. Modest interest-rate hikes with the purpose of pricking what seems to be an asset bubble tend to be insufficient to contain the enthusiasm of those who are in the game for very high expected returns. Aggressive hikes, in turn, can provoke severe damage to the economy. Bernanke concludes that "a far better approach [...] is to use micro-level policies to reduce the incidence of bubbles and to protect the financial system against their effects." (Bernanke, 2002, p. 9).

A very similar view was expressed by Alan Greenspan in a book published one year after he left the Fed. To begin with, the former all-powerful Fed's chairman emphasized how difficult it is to draw the line between the effects on the stock market of a healthy economic boom and a speculative bubble. Besides, he doubted that even if the central bank decided that there was a bubble and wished to let the air out of it that task could be accomplished. He exemplified. "By abruptly raising the rate of interest by, say, 10 percentage points, we could explode any bubble overnight". But that would be devastating. "We'd be like killing the patient to cure the disease". On the other hand, moderate tightening would be counterproductive, "more likely to raise stock prices than to lower them". (Greenspan, 2007, pp. 200-202).

Greenspan concluded that the best thing for the Fed to do would be "to stay with our central goal of stabilizing product and services prices", while seeking to "gain the power and flexibility needed to limit economic damage if there was a crash". In the case of a major market decline, the policy would be "to move aggressively, lowering rates and flooding the system with liquidity to mitigate the economic fallout. But the idea of addressing the stock-market boom directly and preemptively seemed out of our reach". (Greenspan, 2007, p. 202).

Although the above-mentioned argument was made in regard to the stock market, the reasoning was applicable to real-estate bubbles as well. In summary, the idea that asset-price bubbles should not be directly addressed by monetary policy makers became part of the consensus. And Greenspan's position certainly had a great deal of influence on the formation of this consensus.

To complete the picture, there was also consensus on the type of macro models to be used to guide monetary policy. In this case, the conventional wisdom involved the so-called general equilibrium models, the DSGEs. Largely used by central banks in general, those models did not incorporate the possibility of gradual increase in debt, leverage and vulnerability which often lead to financial crisis and excessive output fluctuations. As Mervyn King pointed out, in those (New Keynesian) models, "the treatment of expectations is simplified, and neglects the possibility that expectations themselves may be a source of fluctuations, rather simply reflecting change elsewhere in the economy." (King, 2012, p. 5). In particular, the lack of explicit consideration of credit and banking made the models inadequate for the purpose of better understanding the trade-offs between economic and financial stability.

The crisis and the policy responses

Asset bubbles may not necessarily lead to financial disruptions and large output and employment fluctuations. To a great extent, it all depends on whether the bubble is fed by excessive credit, or not. The episode which involved technology stocks in the beginning of the present century was not supported by excessive leverage and debt. In the wake of the burst of the bubble, the stock market (both the Nasdaq as well more general indexes, like the S&P-500) fell for more than two years, but there was no significant deterioration in the balance sheets of banks. There was a recession, but it was mild and short-lived, lasting less than a year. The period 2001-02 was one of slow growth, but in 2003 the economy was already expanding at its potential rate (2.5% per annum). The Fed reacted to the burst of the bubble by lowering the basic rate, a policy which (due to concerns with deflation) persisted through the middle of 2003, when the federal funds rate reached 1.0%.

But the story may get a lot worse than that if too much credit is involved, as in the recent housing bubble. In such cases, houses and apartments are acquired with the support of credit. The lending institutions receive those items as collaterals for their support. As demand expands, the prices of real estate go up, stimulating further supply of credit. One day, for some reason, the process is interrupted. Prices stabilize and then start to fall. Such decline means lower values of collaterals. At this point financial intermediaries step on the brakes and curtail credit expansion. The economic activity is adversely affected, which leads to further decline in the prices of assets and additional tightening of the credit supply. A recession ensues, generally a lengthy one. Banks, household and firms get stuck with excessive debt, a situation which requires a great deal of time to be corrected. In the present case, the costs incurred in cleaning up after the bursting of the bubble proved to be abnormally high.

To a large number of analysts, the recent credit and housing bubbles was the sole fault of the central banks, particularly the Fed. According to this hypothesis, excessively easy monetary policy (in the US and other regions) would have stimulated leverage and debt in an undesirable way.

In a book called *Getting Off Track*, John Taylor argued that "monetary excesses were the main cause" of the boom and resulting bust of the housing sector in the US. (Taylor, 2009, p. 1). His argument is based on the fact that, between 2002 and early 2006, worried about the possibility of deflation, the Fed had set the policy rate at levels substantially below the ones which would have prevailed if the monetary authorities had not abandoned the historically observed pattern, supposedly given by the so-called Taylor rule.

Low interest rates were certainly a fundamental cause of the crisis. In fact, they stimulated the demand for credit and financial intermediaries and asset managers to take more risk, in their search for higher yields.

But monetary policy may have contributed to the crisis in another way, apart from the question of the level of the policy rate. What we have in mind is the issue of instrument volatility. It is a well-known fact that crises tend to occur in the wake of periods dominated by excessive optimism. As noted above, the Great Moderation meant that recession became a milder and less frequent phenomenon. But to what extent this result was obtained at the cost of activism in excess, particularly in the US, the central bank being too ready to lower the policy rate in response to the first signs of a weakening economic activity? In this case, the Fed would have contributed to the rise of a false sense of security, leading many to believe that economic cycles had been tamed. Difficulties in defining "activism in excess" should not weaken the validity of this argument.

In any case, it would be too simplistic to attribute the crisis to the apparent mismanagement of monetary policy. A major event like the recent one cannot have a single cause. In fact, several other factors seem to have worked in the same direction, at the same time, contributing in their own way to the rapid expansion of credit and the formation of bubbles, in the US and in some other countries.

In this group of factors, one is directly linked to the housing market. As argued by Raghuram Rajan, in the American case, prior to the crisis, it had become a governmental policy to increase the access of the population to housing, especially of low-income people. Easy credit was the instrument for that, a mechanism that, in the words of the author, "has been used as palliative throughout history by governments that are unable to address the deeper anxieties of the middle class directly". (Rajan, 2010, p. 9). The idea that consumption matters more than income might be part of the explanation for such policy.

During the Clinton and Bush administrations, Fannie Mae and Freddie Mac – the two giant-government-sponsored agencies – were stimulated (by means of administrative measures) to support housing finance. Those agencies were in the market buying mortgages that conformed to certain standards, thus allowing the lending institutions they acquired the mortgages from to make more lending. After insuring the mortgages against default, they packed pools of individual loans together and issued mortgage-backed securities (MBS), which could be sold to market participants. The two agencies (later nationalized) also invested in MBSs underwritten by other banking institutions. Expanding their activities was certainly not a difficult task, since the implicit government guarantee allowed them access to funding at lower costs, in comparison to their competitors. (Rajan, 2010, p. 34).

Going back to the idea that crises tend to occur in the wake of periods of excessive enthusiasm, we can recall several other factors which contributed significantly to the wave of extraordinary optimism experienced by the world economy since the middle of the 1980s. Among those factors, and in addition to the already-mentioned belief that the economic cycle had been tamed, we could name the end of the Great Inflation, the persistent decline in the long-term rates of interest observed since that time, and the rapid increase in the degree of financial and trade integration of the world economy, made possible by rapid rates of technological progress. Furthermore, from 1993-94 onward, there was a considerable strengthening of the international banking system, especially in the United States. Banks became better capitalized, delinquency rates fell and loans expanded rapidly. In such a scenario, the rise in asset prices was both cause and reflex of the optimistic wave of that period. Such a combination of a large number of favorable factors seems to be a rare phenomenon. (Senna, 2010, pp. 381-387).

As normally happens in periods of excessive confidence in the future, economic agents became more complacent, acting less rigorously in their analysis of risk-return. Old and risky strategies involving, for example, the mismatching of assets and liabilities, like holding long-term and illiquid assets supported by short-term funding instruments, acquired a huge scale, particularly in the US investment banking industry. The mentioned complacency was certainly reinforced by the prevailing sense that in case of financial difficulties government authorities would be there to help, not only through macroeconomic mechanisms like supplying liquidity and lowering the interest rates, but also in a more direct way, especially in the cases of sufficiently big financial institutions.

The diminished rigor in the analysis of risk involved credit-rating firms as well as institutions responsible for generating and distributing papers in the capital markets. In many cases, conflicts of interest were also a major source of problem. The result was the growing use of complex and non-transparent credit instruments, sold to investors without an economic compensation proportional to the risks incurred. At the same time, official entities – central banks included – in charge of regulating and supervising the financial institutions and markets failed dramatically. In part, they based their attitudes on an unjustifiable belief on the self-regulating capacity of the financial sector. Due to all this, from a certain point onward, and in several parts of the world, the whole financial sector became extremely fragile and vulnerable.

The creation of the euro represented one more factor contributing to the widespread optimistic wave which preceded the crisis. In fact, in itself, the new currency brought about a great deal of enthusiasm, best illustrated by the extraordinary convergence of interest rates across the region. Governments which used to pay a lot more than the Germans to access the financial markets suddenly found themselves obtaining funds at rates very close to those paid by the most reliable issuer in the zone – four years before the creation of the euro, the 10-year sovereign papers issued by Italy, Spain and Portugal, for example, paid 500 basis points more than similar issuances by Germany. As the rates on securities issued by several member countries declined, so did interest rates in general. In the so-called periphery, the dominant sentiment was that a passport to prosperity had just been acquired.

In a rather unavoidable way, private debt started to climb. Households, firms and banks simply jumped at the opportunity to borrow under conditions never seen before. The disappearance of the exchange-rate risk within the area stimulated the borrowing spree, while banks in the center of the region felt encouraged to substantially increase international lending within the zone.

On the monetary side, the one-size-fits-all policy gave extra impulse to the new spending cycle. Soon after the introduction of the euro, the German economy was not in a position to support high rates of interest – economic performance was very modest between the 2nd quarter of 2001 and the 1st quarter of 2005. This may be part of the reason why the European Central Bank (ECB) refrained from stepping on the brakes, which would have been an adequate measure for countries in the periphery. In reality, the policy rate was brought down, from 4.75% in April/01 to 2.0% in June/03, remaining at that level until November/05, when it started being gradually raised once again. Besides the situation in Germany, the low levels of interest rates observed in the international markets, particularly in the US, certainly had its influence on the policy stance adopted by the ECB. In any case, the fact of the matter is that, in real terms, the basic rate of interest became negative for a varying number of years in Greece, Portugal, Ireland, Italy, and Spain. The problems in Greece had more to do with mismanagement of the government accounts, but in Portugal, Ireland and Spain the whole scenario produced an extraordinary increase in private leverage and debt. In Ireland and Spain this was accompanied by housing booms.

It seems then that one cannot attribute the crisis exclusively to the most visible factors, like the apparent mismanagement of monetary policy, particularly in the US, and poor regulation and supervision of financial institutions and markets, in general. Several other elements were at play, simultaneously and in the same direction, in a very rare combination of events.

There is no need to elaborate much on what happened as the expanding cycle came to an end. Here, it suffices to say that, at some point, some debtors started having difficulties in honoring their financial obligations. At the same time, asset prices stabilized and then acquired a declining tendency. As a result, the value of collaterals deteriorated and lenders curtailed the supply of credit. Economic activity was adversely affected, which provoked further decline in asset prices and additional constraints to the expansion of credit. Households and firms realized that they had borrowed in excess while banks and other financial institutions realized that they had exaggerated in their leveraging practices, which is equivalent to say that they had lent too much. In different corners of the world, investors and banks found themselves owners of large amounts of illiquid assets, whose values had deteriorated sharply. Particularly in the US and in Europe, a crisis of confidence ensued within the banking industry. Banks stopped trusting their counterparties. Interbank lending came to a complete halt. The situation was seriously aggravated by the fall of Lehman, in September 2008.

Policy responses varied from country to country. Government and monetary authorities' intervention reached unprecedented levels. In many cases, the Treasury and the central bank acted in conjunction. Generally speaking, the responses included government guarantees for certain financial instruments, capitalization of banks, measures to facilitate the access of banks to liquidity provision by the central banks, supply of liquidity to nonbank financial institutions, etc. Mergers and acquisitions of financial institutions were stimulated by governments, central banks and supervisory agencies. Government expenditures increased in an extraordinary way, resulting in huge fiscal deficits and producing very large increases in the size of government debt.

At the same time, the traditional instrument of monetary policy (the interest rate) was brought down to zero, or almost that. In the US, the zero lower bound was reached in December 2008. At that point, the Fed resorted to a policy known as forward guidance, indicating that future movements in the fed funds rate would only happen in a somewhat distant future. Around the same time, the Fed initiated the purchase of a large volume of agency debt and mortgage backed securities "to provide support to the mortgage and housing markets" (later known as QE1) and announced that in the beginning of the following year a program which would facilitate the extension of credit to households and small business would be implemented. It also announced that the benefits of purchases of long-term Treasury securities were being evaluated. A program along this line was effectively introduced only in November 2010, and became known as QE2. Credit and quantitative easing policies such as those were adopted by other central banks as well, largely affecting the size and the composition of the balance sheet of the monetary authorities. They can be justified when the basic interest rate reaches its lower limit, but seem to be applicable only in crisis time. As to forward guidance mechanisms, they had been used in more normal times, and can be considered part of the regular tool kit of central banks.

The disregarded lessons

Prior to the crisis, policy makers in general did not pay due attention to the credit cycle and the rise in the prices of certain assets. No attempt to contain the financial system's creation of private credit and money was made. And no one talked about balance sheet effects. Among economists, some were clever enough to notice what was going on and made their warnings accordingly, but their ideas did not influence the course of events.

In a way, this is surprising. The economic literature is full of contributions of economists who had clearly identified the problems which tend to occur when the prevailing circumstances stimulate the rapid expansion of credit. In the pre-War period, for example, business cycle theorists were pretty much aware of what Hawtrey called "the inherent instability of credit". (Hawtrey, [1932] 1965, p. 166).

Hawtrey's reasoning can be summarized as follows. When banks increase their lending, economic activity improves and consumers' income and outlay expand. "Once an expansion of demand has been definitely started, says the author, it will proceed by its own momentum. No further encouragement from the banks to borrowers is required". (p. 167). When banks reduce their lending, the "vicious circle" works in the opposite direction. In a more general way, "equilibrium having once been disturbed, the departure from equilibrium tends to grow wider and wider, till some contrary disturbance is interposed". (p. 168). This led Hawtrey to conclude that "in the practical business of credit regulation it is vital to take due account of the inherent instability of credit". (p. 168). Sometimes there would be need to modify the tendency to expansion or contraction, sometimes it would be necessary to reverse it. In short, credit is unstable and needs to be firmly regulated.

As other members of the so-called Austrian School before him, Hayek was a strong believer in the line of reasoning presented above. In reality, he went one step further, and made an attempt to explain the mentioned instability. In his view, the problem had to do with banking systems based on fractional reserves, in which commercial banks work with liabilities redeemable on demand and in the monetary unit whose right of issuance belongs exclusively to another institution (the central bank, in the modern world). Under such structure, commercial banks are suppliers of liquid assets, but they are required to keep liquid in terms of another form of money. This means that they are forced to diminish the pace at which money is created exactly when everybody else is willing to hold more liquid assets. (Hayek [1976] 1990, pp. 91-92). This would be "the chief cause of the instability of the existing credit system, and through it of the wide fluctuations in all economic activity." (p. 106).

A story told by Marriner Eccles illustrates Hayek's point. Before becoming chairman of the Fed (1936-48), Eccles was a banker in the Midwest. In his book of memoirs, he explains that, in order to survive the period of the Great Depression, his institution was forced to adopt a tough credit and collection policy. The public wanted cash. By forcing the liquidation of loans and securities to meet the demands of depositors, he realized that he and other bankers were contributing to drive prices down and thereby making increasingly difficult for debtors to pay back what they owned. Such policy, he adds, was equivalent to a "double loop around the throat of an economy that was already gasping for breath". In short, "seeking individual salvation, we were contributing to collective ruin". (Eccles, 1951, pp. 70-71).

As already noted, prior to the recent crisis, at least implicitly, many believed that macroeconomic stability would guarantee financial stability. But could it not be the other way around? What if macroeconomic stability leads to an extraordinary optimistic wave, which results in excessive risk taking, skyrocketing asset prices, too much credit, and a fragile and vulnerable financial system?

In this respect, history has already taught us a lot. There are many examples of crisis preceded by periods of economic stability and excess optimism. The Great Depression may be considered one of these examples. In the *Monetary History*, the period 1921-29 was dubbed by Friedman and Schwartz the "high tide" phase of the Fed. In a later (and more popular) book, co-authored by his wife, Friedman returned to the subject. In his own words, during the mentioned period, the Fed worked as "an effective balance wheel, increasing the rate of monetary growth when the economy showed signs of faltering, and reducing the rate of monetary growth when the economy started expanding more rapidly. It did not prevent fluctuations in the economy but it did contribute to keeping them mild. Moreover, it was sufficiently evenhanded so that it avoided inflation. The result of the stable monetary and economic climate was rapid economic growth. It was widely trumpeted that a new era had arrived, that the business cycle was dead, dispatched by a vigilant Federal Reserve System." (Friedman and Friedman, 1980, p. 78). One cannot escape the following conclusion: something quite similar to the Great Moderation had been experienced before.

The idea of a stable macro scenario leading to an extraordinary optimistic wave, fueled by credit, and degenerating into a financial crisis is largely associated with the name of Hyman Minsky, according to whom a full-employment situation is not sustainable. When it is achieved, "businessmen and bankers, heartened by success, tend to accept larger doses of debt-financing". During periods of tranquil expansions, his argument continues, new financial instruments are created. "Full employment is a transitory state because speculation upon and experimentation with liability structures and novel financial assets will lead the economy to an investment boom. An investment boom leads to inflation, and [...] an inflationary boom leads to a financial structure that is conducive to financial crisis." (Minsky, [1986] 2008, p. 199).

In his well-known book *Manias, Panics and Crashes*, Charles Kindleberger takes Minsky's "model" as the starting point of his analysis. "According to Minsky – says the author –, events leading up to a crisis start with a 'displacement', some exogenous, outside shock to the macroeconomic system. The nature of the displacement varies from one speculative boom to another. [...] But whatever the source of the displacement, if it is sufficiently large and pervasive, it will alter the economic outlook by changing profit opportunities in at least one important sector of the economy. [...] If the new opportunities dominate [...], investment and production pick up. A boom is under way [...] and is fed by an expansion of credit which enlarges the total money supply". (Kindleberger, 1978, pp. 15-16).

"After a time, the argument continues, increased demand presses against the capacity to produce goods or the supply of existing financial assets. Prices increase, giving rise to new profit opportunities and attracting still further firms and investors. [...] At this stage we may well get what Minsky calls 'euphoria' [...] and Adam Smith and his contemporaries called 'overtrading'. [...] When the number of firms and households indulging in these practices grows large [...] speculation for profits leads away from normal, rational behavior to what have been described as 'manias' or 'bubbles'. The word 'mania' emphasizes the irrationality; 'bubble' foreshadows the bursting". (Kindleberger, 1978, pp. 16-17).

More recently, for almost a decade prior to the crisis, researchers at the Bank for International Settlements (BIS) called attention for the need to avoid excessive credit creation and financial instability. Andrew Crockett was the General Manager of the Bank from 1994 until March 2003. In a speech made in Hong Kong, in February 2001, he observed that the existing conceptual framework for the promotion of financial stability was inadequate, since it did not pay sufficient attention to the genesis of financial instability.

Crockett was particularly concerned with the fact that "the pursuit of price stability can sometimes allow financial imbalances to arise inadvertently, and can sow the seeds of subsequent instability". He was also worried about the approach taken by regulators and supervisors, who looked at financial stability from the micro point of view. According to his thought, "the pursuit of prudential objectives, institution by institution, can take inadequate account of feedback mechanisms that can exacerbate macroeconomic cycles". (Crockett, 2001, p. 3).

In Crockett's view, there would be numerous cases in which the restoration of price stability provided fertile ground for excessive optimism, which would take asset prices to unrealistic levels. "In a stylized financial cycle, he argues, some exogenous development sets off an expansion of credit. It is often improved economic prospects, due to technological innovation, the implementation of reforms, or indeed many other genuine, real factors. Once under way, credit expansion fuels an acceleration of output and an increase in asset prices. Such developments appear to boost returns and lower risk, leading to further credit expansion and increased leverage in the system. If the mechanisms of prudential oversight [...] work well, excessive leverage will be avoided. [...] But if the extension of balance sheets goes too far, an eventual reversal can be abrupt and severe, with widespread bankruptcies, and substantial damage to financial intermediaries". (Crockett, 2001, p. 4).

Among those who were investigating the points raised by Crockett within the BIS, one can single out the name of Claudio Borio, who, co-authored by several other researchers, has been writing on those themes ever since the beginning of the years 2000. In a working paper dated July 2002, for example, Borio and Philip Lowe were already defending a system-wide focus on the prevention of crises, together with a greater willingness of monetary authorities to respond to the occasional development of financial imbalances that might pose a threat to the health of the economy. (Borio and Lowe, 2002).

In summary, it became common to hear (or read) people talking about the "lessons from the crisis". For sure, one can always learn from events as important as the recent ones. But it seems fair to say that the major and more general lessons were already taught by the history of financial crises, examined by a considerable number of economic historians. It makes more sense, then, to talk about "disregarded lessons".

The future of central banking

The inflation targeting framework which prevailed before the crisis was based on two fundamental ideas, namely: a) inflation is a monetary phenomenon and b) there is no permanent trade-off between inflation and unemployment. This means that a central bank cannot permanently affect the behavior of real variables. All that it can achieve is low and stable inflation. And this is the task a monetary authority should be dedicated to. In pursuing this objective, however, the central bank must preserve the flexibility to offset cyclical deviations in economic activity and employment. In other words, in the conduct of monetary policy, due consideration should be given to the short-term behavior of the real economy. Other key principles of the IT framework were credibility, predictability and transparency of the decision-making process. Good communication is of fundamental importance.

The above-mentioned characteristics have been part of successful monetary policy experiences for longer than it appears, since they became essential ingredients of the monetary targeting regime adopted in Germany and Switzerland from the mid-1970s onward. As pointed out earlier in this article, the IT practitioners simply incorporated those traits into a new framework, based on a different type of anchor to the price system. It seems, then, that the aforementioned set of ideas and principles is what really works in terms of monetary policy strategy. And the crisis did not destroy their validity.

Putting it in another way, none of the recent events suggests that it is unwise for central banks to adopt a strong and credible commitment to stabilizing the rate of inflation in the medium and long run by making explicit a numerical inflation objective, while at the same time preserving the flexibility to take into account the behavior of the real economy, being ready to postpone the convergence of inflation to the target in the presence of certain types of shock. Experience has shown that inflation rates may fluctuate, but as long as the central bank is sufficiently credible, economic agents expect them to return to target. In an environment of well-anchored inflationary expectations, shocks like those associated with exchange-rate depreciations and oil and commodity price rises tend to have less-permanent effects on the inflation rate. By now, there is ample evident of the validity of these assertions. And, therefore, there is no objective reason for abandoning the essence of inflation targeting, as indeed no one has done so far.

But in one aspect things are bound to change in the world of central banking, or are already changing. The preservation of financial stability requires a great deal more of attention. In addressing this issue in a conference held in 2011, Bernanke put it this way: "central banks certainly did not ignore issues of financial stability in the decades before the recent crisis, but financial stability policy was often viewed as the junior partner to monetary policy". He concluded that "one of the most important legacies of the crisis will be the restoration of financial stability policy to co-equal status with monetary policy". (Bernanke, 2011, p. 5).

It seems then that the real question is how central banks should deal with the problem of financial stability. To a large extent this problem involves avoiding excessive leverage and risk taking as well as the formation of asset price bubbles. If we concentrate our attention on credit-driven bubbles, the mentioned task presupposes some capacity to identify situations in which excess credit is being created and asset prices are diverting from fundamentals. Experience has taught how difficult this is.

Independently from the difficulties involved, there are two possible approaches to the mentioned problem. And one does not necessarily exclude the other. The first one has to do with monetary policy being geared to lean against movements in credit aggregates or asset prices. In this case, the policy rate would be used with the purpose of guaranteeing financial stability besides its regular objectives of minimizing the variability of output and inflation from the respective targets.

The issue is an old one, as already noted. In essence, it is necessary to bear in mind that during a self-reinforcing cycle of optimism and credit expansion a large number of market participants expect to obtain quite high rates of return in one or more asset market. This means that they become insensitive to any reasonable increase in interest rates. Fifty years ago, Friedman and Schwartz argued that, in such a scenario, any palatable change in monetary policy is bound to be too timid to break the boom and too restrictive to promote a healthy macroeconomic picture. In other words, leaning against a credit or asset bubble might result in a weaker economy and/or inflation below target, with no guarantee of success in terms of pricking the bubble. If something of this sort happens, the central bank might lose its credibility. Opting for this alternative would be like taking a bet, something that central bankers are not supposed to do.

Another argument equally unfavorable to the "leaning against" alternative has to do with the fact that any announcement that the monetary authorities manage the policy rate with a third objective in mind (promoting financial stability) besides the traditional ones of correcting deviations of output and inflation from targets might destroy the beauty of the inflation targeting regime, namely, its clarity and simplicity. After all, the public would ask: what is it exactly that the central bank pursues? What does the policy rate really aim at? There would be no clear-cut signal.

The trade-off between macroeconomic stability and financial stability contributes to make the "lean against" a non-viable alternative. The difficulties lie in the fact that we have two objectives and just one policy instrument. Perhaps, then, the solution would be to resort to the "separation principle" proposed by Tinbergen, who, decades ago, argued that in order to achieve a given number of policy targets we cannot work with a smaller number of instruments.

This brings us to the second possible approach, around which some sort of a consensus is being formed. In this case, the interest rate takes care of macro stability and macro-prudential measures take care of financial stability.

In principle, those who favor this sort of combination admit (at least implicitly) that identifying a credit-driven bubble is not as difficult as one might think. To accomplish this task, the authorities must check the behavior of variables like the stock of credit, the leverage of financial institutions, risk spreads, asset prices, etc. To the extent allowed by data availability, information on households and firms' degree of indebtedness might also be quite useful.

In any discussion of this second approach, the first thing to notice is that macro-prudential measures can be of different types. They can seek to contain the actions of borrowers, or they can be conceived to influence the behavior of lenders. Limits on loan-to-value ratios are an example of the first type. Dynamic provisioning for losses by banks and countercyclical capital requirements are examples of the second. Furthermore, measures like these can be built into the rules, which obviously imply previous agreements, or they can be adopted on an ad hoc basis, implemented as the authorities feel appropriate. The list of instruments may also include controls on international capital flows.

If we have in mind the prevention of bubbles, we need to talk about restrictive macro-prudential measures. And here is exactly where the problem lies. As it is widely known, removing the punch bowl before the party is over is usually complicated. The mentioned expression has been used in regard to a tightening of monetary policy (raising the rate of interest when everybody is still enjoying the party), but it is probably even more applicable to the case of prudential tightening. The reason has to do with the fact that changes in macro-prudential tools have effects which tend to be more concentrated than those produced by changes in the conduction of monetary policy.

Let us assume, for example, that the competent authorities have objective reasons to believe that a given expansion of credit is going too far, with a tendency to provoke serious imbalances, and decide to curb such development. Let us assume that restricting the purchase of housing is what they decide to do. People potentially affected by this action will certainly react. The same reasoning would apply if the authorities considered restraining the expansion of credit. Measures taken with this objective usually have a direct impact on banks' profits and, again, are likely to be met with resistance. Those benefiting from the growth of credit are also likely to complain about the imposition of restrictions. The point here is not that the authorities would necessarily be hampered from doing what they wished, but that they would be reluctant to act. The costs of leaning against an optimistic wave are always present. Besides the fact that most of the (supposedly) necessary measures are bound to be met with resistance, one cannot forget that the diagnosis is never precise and the results of the actions are normally quite uncertain.

One solution to this could be to negotiate with the interested parties beforehand, incorporating the desired changes into new rules for the banking system, for example. But this too is bound to be met with resistance. Once again, the reason has to do with the impact that the conceived measures might have on banks' profits. In addition, one may wish to take measures capable of diminishing the pro-cyclical nature of banking activities or strengthening the balance sheets of banks during good times, so that they are better positioned to face bad times. Dynamic provisioning for losses by banks and countercyclical capital requirements are examples of measures in these directions. The big problem here is how to define "good times".

The so-called Basel III agreement is frequently cited as an indicator of progress in the field of banking regulation. The agreement is the result of efforts by representatives from 27 countries (banking supervisory authorities and monetary policy makers) who took part in a series of meetings sponsored by The Bank for International Settlements (BIS). Within the group there has been a consensus on the need to strengthen the banking institutions in general. The committee set up to define new rules has already emerged with a large number of recommendations. In essence, such recommendations aim at enlarging the capacity of banking institutions to absorb losses and at diminishing the risks of contagion in times of crisis. There has been an increase in the requirements of capital of better quality, while institutions considered to be important from the point of view of systemic risk are supposed to hold an even greater capital base. Furthermore, two additional types of supplementary capital are contemplated. They are called buffers, one designated by conservation, and the other meant to be of a counter-cyclical nature. The introduction of a leverage index, viewed as a complement to the obligation of minimum capital, is also part of the recommendations, and so is the maintenance of some liquidity requirements. Details on how these last two proposals would work as well as the allocation of additional capital to institutions considered to be systemically important are still the object of negotiations.

The adjustments proposed under the Basel III agreement will be implemented in a gradual way. They will be completed in 2019, when the ordinary minimum capital requirement will reach 7.0%., a figure which already includes the conservation buffer (2.5%). The counter-cyclical buffer will oscillate between zero and 2.5%, at the discretion of the national authorities, which have until 2015 to decide. According the guidelines supplied by the committee deviations from its long run trend of the credit to GDP ratio should be one of the criteria for the building up of reserves. No doubt, the new requirements represent a considerable improvement if compared to the rules embodied into the previous agreement (Basel II), according to which the capital base in conditions of absorbing losses was only 2.0%.

As we can see, there has been a considerable progress in regard to the strengthening of the capital base of the banking institutions. Agreement on this matter was certainly facilitated by the understanding that the previously existing capital base was too low. As regards other aspects of the agreement, progress has not been as good. In fact, there is a substantial number of pending issues, which makes it difficult to predict how effective the mechanisms that will really be approved will be.

In any case, it is important to stress that improvements in the rules under which the banks operate certainly facilitate the actions of the central bankers. Policy makers, however, are likely to want more than that. They normally wish to preserve some leeway to act on a discretionary basis, in response to the needs of the moment. And it seems to be to the approach based on Tinbergen's principle that they are heading for. This appears to be the preference of academic economists as well.

To the extent that the idea of having two instruments to reach two distinct objectives really prevails, it is crucial to notice the importance of policy coordination. This is especially so due to the fact that although each of the two instruments tends to have a stronger impact on the target it has been assigned to, it is capable of affecting the other objective as well. In other words, changes in the policy rate have the capacity to influence the behavior of aggregate credit and asset prices, for example, while measures that restrain the growth of credit affect aggregate demand and, in consequence, economic activity and the prices of goods and services.

No doubt, this sort of policy coordination is bound to be an issue for the years to come. A great deal of research will certainly be conducted with the objective of making such coordination effective. At the moment, what we know is that it seems to be wise to deliver the two policies to the same government agency. Fortunately, this appears to be the way things are going.

In 2010, in the United States, the so-called Dodd-Frank act attributed greater responsibilities to the Fed in the area of financial stability. The central bank is now in charge of supervising the operations of non-bank financial institutions considered to be systemically important by the Financial Stability Oversight Council. In addition to this, due to its own initiative, the Fed has already reoriented its supervisory activities in such a way as to incorporate issues related to systemic risks. (Bernanke, 2011, pp. 10-11). In 1997, in the UK, the responsibility for banking supervision was removed from the Bank of England and given to a new regulator, the Financial Services Authority. A law approved in 2012 reverted this movement, giving the mentioned function back to the Bank. An independent committee was created, with the objective of identifying, monitoring and acting to remove or reduce systemic risks. Within the Bank of England, there are now two committees of equal importance: the Monetary Policy Committee and the Financial Policy Committee. In the euro zone, the movement is the same. An European Systemic Risk Board was created with the purpose of identifying, prioritizing and calling attention to situations which might pose systemic risks. Under the command of the president of the European Central Bank, the Board makes recommendations (to the national authorities) on macro-prudential measures.

Although the available signs indicate that the future of central banking will no longer involve the problematic dichotomy between monetary and financial stability policies, we are far from knowing whether we are really heading in the right direction. In particular, although macro-prudential measures are likely to gain in importance as a new policy lever to deal with apparent financial imbalances, we still do not know whether they could do the job as adequately as desired. As Blanchard and others have recently put it, we still do not know how they interact with other policies. In short, we are "a long way from knowing how to use them reliably". (Blanchard et al., 2013, p. 17).

As Bernanke said in the conclusion of his 2011 paper, it "must be viewed as provisional" the consensus that is being formed around the approach based on Tinbergen's principle, according to which central banks can dedicate separate toolkits to achieving their financial stability and macroeconomic objectives. (Bernanke, 2011, p. 14).

References

Bernanke, Ben S., 2002, "Asset-Price Bubbles and Monetary Policy", speech at The National Association for Business Economics, October 15.

Bernanke, Ben S., 2011, "The Effects of the Great Recession on Central Bank Doctrine and Practice", 56th Economic Conference, Federal Reserve Bank of Boston, October 18.

Bernanke, Ben S., Laubach, Thomas, Mishkin, Frederic S., and Posen, Adam, 1999, *Inflation Targeting – Lessons from the International Experience*. Princeton: Princeton University Press.

Blanchard, Olivier, Dell'Ariccia, Giovanni and Mauro, Paolo, 2013, "Rethinking Macro Policy II: Getting Granular", IMF Staff Discussion Note, April 15.

Borio, Claudio and Lowe, Philip, 2002, "Asset Prices, Financial and Monetary Stability: Exploring the Nexus", BIS Working Paper no. 114, July.

Crockett, Andrew, 2001, "Monetary Policy and Financial Stability", the Fourth HKMA Distinguished Lecture, Hong Kong, February 13.

Eccles, Marriner S., 1951, *Beckoning Frontiers*. New York: Alfred A. Knoff.

Friedman, Milton, 1968, "The Role of Monetary Policy". *The American Economic Review*, vol. 58, n.1, March.

Friedman, Milton and Friedman, Rose, 1980, *Free to Choose*. New York: Harcourt Brace Jovanovich.

Friedman, Milton and Schwartz, Anna, 1963, *A Monetary History of the United States, 1867-1960*. Princeton: Princeton University Press.

Greenspan, Alan, 2007, *The Age of Turbulence*. New York: The Penguin Press.

Hamilton, James D., 1987, "Monetary Factors in the Great Depression". *Journal of Monetary Economics*, vol. 19, no. 2, March.

Hawtrey, R. G., [1932] 1965, *The Art of Central Banking*. New York: Augustus M. Kelley.

Hayek, Friedrich A., [1976] 1990, *Denationalisation of Money – the Argument Refined*. London; Institute of Economic Affairs.

Issing, Otmar, 2012, "Central Banks – Paradise Lost", the Mayekawa Lecture, Institute for Monetary and Economic Studies, Bank of Japan, May 30.

Johnson, Harry, 1971, "The Keynesian Revolution and the Monetarist Counter-Revolution". *The American Economic Review*, vol. 61, no. 1, May.

Keynes, John M., [1930] 1950, *A Treatise on Money, vol. II*. London: Macmillan and Co.

Kindleberger, Charles P., 1978, *Manias, Panics and Crashes*. New York: Basic Books.

King, Mervyn, 2012, "Twenty Years of Inflation Targeting", The Stamp Memorial Lecture, London School of Economics, October 9.

Minsky, Hyman P., [1986] 2008, *Stabilizing an Unstable Economy*. New York: McGraw Hill.

Mishkin, Frederic S., 2012, "Central Banking After the Crisis", paper prepared for the 16th Annual Conference of the Central Bank of Chile, Santiago, Chile, November 15 and 16.

Rajan, Raghuram G., 2010, *Fault Lines*. Princeton: Princeton University Press.

Senna, José Júlio, 2010, *Política Monetária – Ideias, Experiências e Evolução*. Rio de Janeiro: FGV Editora.

Taylor, John B., 2009, *Getting Off Track*. Stanford: Hoover Institution Press.

White, William R., 2012, "Ultra Easy Monetary Policy and the Law of Unintended Consequences", Federal Reserve Bank of Dallas, Globalization and Monetary Policy Institute, Working Paper No. 126, September.

3

The costs of inflation

Under the gold-standard system, the price level oscillated in the short run, but it was relatively stable over the medium and the long term. After World War II, when the whole world migrated – apparently in a definitive way – to fiduciary money, inflation became a potential problem. After all, previous experiences with fiat money (some of which were temporary abandonments of the metallic system) had led to very rapid rates of price increases, normally accompanied by severe economic difficulties. As Irving Fisher once put it, "irredeemable paper money has almost invariably proved a curse to the country employing it". (Fisher, [1911] 1963, p. 131).

Perhaps surprisingly, inflation did not become an issue in the immediate post-war period. On the one hand, prices were not rising fast in any major economy. On the other, the then dominant economic paradigm – Keynesianism – did not have a theory of inflation. The fact of the matter is that inflation did not turn into a subject normally discussed by economists.

The inflationary phenomenon was introduced into the main body of economic analysis only after the birth of the Phillips Curve, in 1958, when A. W. Phillips showed an empirical relation between the unemployment rate and the rate of nominal wage change. The work involved data for the United Kingdom, covering the period 1861-1957. (Phillips, 1958).

Soon after the publication of that paper, Paul Samuelson and Robert Solow reproduced the same sort of study for the US economy, using annual rates of price growth rather than nominal wage variations. (Samuelson-Solow, 1960). The authors were aware of the fact that the curve could shift and have its shape modified over time. Nevertheless, they made use of the expression "menu of choice" and somehow stimulated the notion that a trade-off was there to be exploited.

In the following years, the idea that by accepting higher inflation economic policy makers could obtain a permanently lower rate of unemployment became somewhat widespread. Behind this reasoning was some sort of a disregard for the costs of inflation and, as shown below, the belief that whatever the costs they could be largely mitigated by indexation.

The traditional approach

In any discussion on the costs of inflation, it is necessary to make the distinction between unanticipated and anticipated inflation. In the past there were numerous cases of unanticipated inflation associated with wars and serious domestic conflicts. World War I is a case in point. Struggling for resources to finance the war effort, countries involved in the conflict abandoned the gold standard and resorted to the printing of fiat money. Most of them did so in a gigantic scale. The general price level increased tremendously, a phenomenon which ended up affecting economies not directly involved in the dispute. In some countries (the UK, the US and Canada, for example) prices went continuously up until the end of the War and fell during the following years. In others, like Germany, they acquired an explosive trend.

The episode was analyzed by Keynes in his 1923 book, *A Tract on Monetary Reform*. To illustrate the magnitude of the problem, the author put together a series of statistics provided by the old League of Nations. Between 1914 and 1920, wholesale prices tripled in the UK and more than doubled in the US and Canada. In France and Italy they increased more than five and six-fold, respectively. In Germany, the early 1920's was a period of hyperinflation. (Keynes, [1923] 2000, p. 3).

To fully understand the nature of the problem one must realize that a large number of the economies affected by the inflationary phenomenon used to operate under the assumption of price stability. Individuals and firms were not prepared for those absurd changes in the value of money. Under this circumstance, a rapid rise in prices generates a wealth-redistribution process of a random nature. Wealth is transferred from one person to another without any particular criterion. In the mentioned episode, particularly troublesome was the enormous destruction of private wealth. As pointed out by Keynes, in Europe, pre-war savings invested in bonds, mortgages and bank deposits were largely or entirely wiped out by the War and the monetary policy which accompanied and followed it. (Keynes, [1923] 2000, pp. 13-14).

Decades later, when economists started to get deeper into the problem of the costs of inflation, it became common to consider the arbitrary redistributions of income and wealth associated with unexpected inflation the main cost of such a phenomenon.

Unexpected inflation redistributes wealth from nominal creditors to nominal debtors. At first sight, since the governmental sector is a great debtor in most or all countries, there might be a tendency to believe that the issue is purely one of wealth transfers between the private sector, on the one hand, and the government, on the other. However, one must realize that, to the extent that government debts are largely issued in nominal terms, unexpected inflation reduces the real value of the stock of debt and this means that the amount of future tax payments required to service or retire the debt is accordingly reduced. Younger and future generations tend to benefit, while older generations are liable to lose. Current owners of the national debt are harmed by inflation to the benefit of future taxpayers. In this case, we have basically a question of intergenerational transfer of wealth.

As to income redistributions, important examples are those involving wages and profits. In consequence of unexpected inflation, recipients of profit income may be benefited at the expense of wage earners. A similar phenomenon might occur between those who pay rents, on the one hand, and those who receive rents, on the other. In the private credit market it is the same. Given that inflation is not expected, loan agreements tend to be specified in nominal terms. If inflation comes as a surprise, the ex-post real rate of interest will differ from what both parties expected. One party will lose and the other will win.

What are the welfare costs of such redistributions? To begin with, most people are risk averse, that is to say, they dislike uncertainty. The unpredictability of the final results can thus be considered harmful to almost everyone. One may argue, however, that gains and losses associated with unanticipated inflation tend to cancel out over the economy as a whole. If we did not care about redistributing wealth and income among individuals, the costs of unanticipated inflation could be viewed as minor. But things are not that simple. Poor segments of the population might be hurt to the benefit of the rich, which would be unfair. And this is a big problem once we realize that political stability requires the economic system of any economy to be perceived (by the public at large) as basically fair.

In any case, independently from who loses and who wins, the random character of the problem is always present. The mentioned redistributions can be considered costly to society mainly because they mean that income and wealth are transferred on a random basis. Keynes emphasized the role of wealth redistributions and the loss of legitimacy such redistributions imply for capitalist institutions.

Economists started to go deeper into the costs-of-inflation issue in the late 1970s and the first half of the next decade. In a series of papers published during that period, Stanley Fischer dedicated himself to the theme. (Fischer 1981, 1984). In the first of those articles he had Franco Modigliani as his co-author. (Fischer and Modigliani 1978). The approach originally adopted, and maintained in subsequent works, involved organizing the discussion by means of a listing of the major real effects of inflation. The usefulness of such an approach leads us to maintain it in the present essay. The list of costs includes: a) welfare losses; b) menu costs; c) price level uncertainty; d) relative price variability; and e) non-adaptation of the tax system.

Welfare losses

A couple of decades before Fischer and Modigliani started organizing the discussion by listing the main components of the costs of inflation, Martin Bailey wrote on the welfare losses provoked by inflationary finance. (Bailey 1956). All subsequent studies on the subject incorporated Bailey's approach.

Bailey starts out by assuming that a given and unchanged rate of inflation is expected by everyone, after the government communicates the monetary policy it intends to follow. He further assumes that cost-of-living adjustments are then made and bank deposits are negligible. By making these hypotheses the author wishes to show that the welfare costs are independent from the distributive and disruptive aspects of inflation and cannot be avoided by sliding-scale arrangements or by foreknowledge of the course of prices.

In Bailey's analysis it is also assumed that the demand for real cash balances is a stable function of the nominal rate of interest. There is an initial desired amount of real money. When the government announces inflation the nominal rate of interest goes up and hence raises the opportunity cost of holding cash. In consequence, the demand for real money balances diminishes. The excess is used in the acquisition of goods and services.

To the extent that the announced money growth is pursued on a sustained basis (as assumed in Bailey's example) there will be inflation over the short and the long run. Interest rates and real cash balances will be lower. It is worth noticing that for the stock of real cash balances to diminish, the price level must rise faster than the volume of money, for some time. For a while, inflation is higher than the long-run inflation rate.

The destruction of real cash balances provoked by the announcement of inflation represents a cost to society. (Bailey 1956, p. 110). There is an aggregate loss of utility which can be represented by an area (a triangle) under the demand for money. By adjusting their cash balances to a lower level, people have to make more frequent trips to the bank. We can think of this cost as equivalent to the inconveniences that people suffer as they economize on money balances. Sometimes this is called the shoe-leather cost of inflation.

As the original non-inflationary environment is permanently transformed into one in which there is a constant rate of price growth, the public will be willing to maintain the reduced stock of real money balances. The inconveniences caused by such reduction will be present period after period. So, in comparison to a situation characterized by price stability, inflation provokes a permanent cost, which cannot be removed by institutional adaptation. However, as transaction technology changes, this cost falls. With the intense use of debit and credit cards, observed in recent times, the tendency is for this cost to become negligible.

Bailey's analysis shows that inflation involves not only a cost, represented by the destruction of real cash balances, but also a tax. This tax is different from all others but has similar effects. To see this, one must recall that a sustained growth of the money supply implies a permanent rate of inflation. For the sake of simplicity, we can assume no real income growth. This means that in the long run the public is willing to hold a constant stock of real cash balances – if the inflation rate is constant, so is the nominal level of the interest rate. Given the presence of rising prices, the maintenance of the real value of the money balances requires the public to increase the stock of nominal balances at a rate capable of offsetting the impact of inflation. For this to happen, individuals have to divert part of their income to raise their holdings of nominal money. This effort is simply an attempt to avoid the deterioration of the real value of their stocks of real money. The relevant point is that the desire to maintain such stock constant means that part of people's income cannot be spent. In summary, the government spends more and the public less, just as would happen in case the extra governmental expenditures were financed by regular taxation.

In real terms, the proceeds of this tax are equivalent to the rate of inflation multiplied by the stock of real cash balances. The effect does not differ from that of a direct tax on the holding of money. (Bailey 1956, p. 94). We can then say that the inconveniences that people suffer are the result of their attempt to escape the inflationary tax.

Menu costs

Menu costs are those associated with the physical costs of changing prices. In the presence of inflation, firms need to modify their posted prices with some frequency. In principle, the higher the rate of inflation, the more often they have to do so. And this involves printing and distributing new catalogs. In the case of restaurants, it involves printing new menus, hence the way this cost is normally identified.

Price level uncertainty

In their 1978 paper, Fischer and Modigliani called attention for the fact that "there is no necessary link between the rate of inflation and the variability of the inflation rate". They added, however, that, apparently, "the variability of the rate of inflation [...] increases with the level of inflation". (Fisher and Modigliani 1978, p. 828).

An empirical investigation of this last statement was conducted by Fischer in his 1984 article. At the occasion, the author presented a graph in which he plotted CPI rates of inflation against the variability of the rate of inflation, measured by its variance. The sample covered the period 1973-1983 and included only OECD countries. Although a simple look at the graph allows one to notice a number of cases of high-inflation economies with relatively inflation variability, the conclusion was that "the empirical evidence is that there is more uncertainty about future price levels at high than at low average rates of inflation". (Fischer 1984, pp. 38-39).

Even assuming that people can predict short-run inflation, long-term inflation cannot be foreseen. In reality, the higher the rate of inflation (current and expected rates for the near future), the more insecure people tend to be. In economies with long tradition of price stability, or very low inflation rates, this sense of uneasiness does not exist.

The point is that significant uncertainty about the price level which will prevail in the future implies costs to society. Even if indexed assets are available, this simply reduces the costs to the public associated with long-run uncertainty about the price level, but it does not eliminate it. Such uncertainty diverts people's attention from productive activities. Individuals and firms are compelled to spend a great deal of time and effort in attempting to manage the inflationary risk. A second source of cost has to do with the tendency for individuals and firms to shorten their time horizons and contracts. A third one relates to the increased attractiveness of real assets as hedges against inflation, particularly real estate and assets denominated in foreign currencies.

One important consequence of all this might be a decline in the savings and investment rates. In the financial sector, the shortening of horizons implies a reduction in the average maturity of the sources of funding available to the banking industry, forcing banks to avoid long-term financing. This is detrimental to the process of physical-capital accumulation. The higher the rate of inflation, the more important these considerations tend to be.

In the graph below we provide further evidence of the relation between the level of inflation and its variability. The exercise is based on IMF data and involves a sample of 128 countries, covering the period between 1980 and 2012. Economies which experienced average rates of price growth higher than 25% per annum (a total of 38) were not included in the sample. We can see from the graph that the higher the average rate of inflation, the greater the variance, especially for rates of inflation higher than 10.0% per annum. Such a relation holds for the highly inflationary economies as well (not shown).

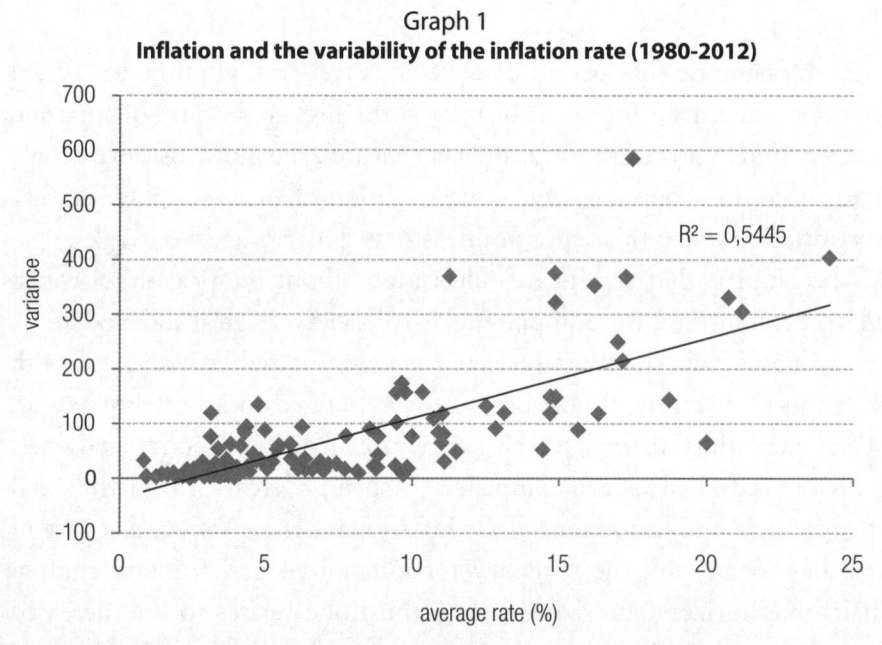

Graph 1
Inflation and the variability of the inflation rate (1980-2012)

$R^2 = 0{,}5445$

Note: sample of 128 countries with average inflation rates below 25% per annum. Source: WEO/IMF

Relative price variability

In market economies, the price system plays a crucial role. Market prices convey information on consumers' preferences and product scarcities. In such economies, resources are allocated in response to movements in relative prices. To the extent that the system works freely, resources tend to be allocated in an efficient way.

The efficiency of the system is damaged, however, in the presence of significant inflation. The reason is that, in such case, it becomes harder for economic agents to distinguish price movements arising from general inflation from movements caused by changes in demand and supply conditions. The quality of the signals sent by the price system deteriorates.

Over the long run, efficiency in the allocation of resources is of fundamental importance for the economic growth process of any economy. This means that inflation may hurt the growth process. High inflation implies greater uncertainty about the price level as well as greater uncertainty about relative prices. Inflation not only shortens economic agents' time horizons and affects decisions to save and invest, but it also causes microeconomic inefficiencies. These problems may substantially reduce the pace of economic growth. However, in spite of the great deal of research that has been done on the possible relation between inflation and economic growth, the results are still inconclusive. To the extent that one agrees on the causality, one important question to which there is no consensual response has to do with the level of inflation beyond which the inflationary process starts hurting economic growth.

Non-adaptation of the tax system

In the real world, people normally think in nominal terms. Indexed assets and contracts are not uncommon, but indexation is usually restricted and tax codes, in particular, are not adapted to changes in the value of money. At least, they are not entirely adapted. This is true even in economies which have experienced high rates of inflation for long periods of time.

Governments are reluctant to fully index their economies for understandable reasons. First, decisions in such a direction might be viewed as an expression of failure. Second, indexation might increase the tolerance to inflation. Third, as regards tax codes, governments benefit by avoiding that sort of adaptation, since in such case inflation increases the real value of individual's tax liabilities.

The major distortions caused by lack of adaptation of the tax codes can be explained as follows. First of all, if nominal income brackets are not adequately corrected, inflation moves individuals into higher income-tax groups. This leads to the taxation of nominal income gains and thus reduces real disposable income. Secondly, capital gains are usually taxed based on the differences between the prices at which assets are sold and the prices at which they were originally acquired, without allowing for the monetary correction of these ones. Taxes are levied on nominal gains. Thirdly, to the extent that the corporate income tax legislation is progressive, inflation shifts firms into higher income groups. In this case, the problem of taxing nominal profits is aggravated by the fact that estimates of depreciation are usually based on the unadjusted value of fixed assets. The same is true as regards the lack of monetary correction of the firm's capital base. These factors reduce the real rate of return to the shareholders and work as a disincentive to savings and capital formation. Additionally, such distortions give rise to a sense of injustice and stimulate tax evasion.

Could we conclude from this discussion that high inflation would be perfectly acceptable as long as we made use of extensive indexation? After all, indexation would eliminate a great deal of the distortions caused by inflation. Should it be considered an adequate substitute for price stability?

Abstracting from the usual reluctance to adopt it, and noting that full indexation is neither possible nor desirable, extensive indexation is indeed capable of eliminating a good number of the distortionary effects of inflation. But other costs would remain. And these are: a) the so-called shoe-lather costs; b) menu costs; c) aggregate price level uncertainty; and d) relative price uncertainty. The first two ones cannot be considered particularly relevant in the modern world, but the last two ones are of great importance. Indexation would not make them disappear. Inflation uncertainty would still be present and the price system would still work with reduced efficiency.

At a more technical level, one can raise several objections to indexation. One of them has to do with the fact that it reduces the flexibility of the economy to deal with supply shocks, especially if wages are indexed. Another one relates to the loss of efficacy of demand management policies associated with the fact that indexation increases the persistence of inflation. The inertial component, which is present in any inflationary process, becomes even more important. The more one prepares the economy to live with inflation, the bigger this problem becomes. In this case, anti-inflationary policies become a lot more costly, for fiscal and monetary tightening produces smaller effects on inflation and greater impact on economic activity. The introduction of mechanisms which supposedly make life easier under inflation tends to increase the tolerance to rapid rates of price growth. The increased cost of combating inflation operates in the same direction. Both factors contribute to the perpetuation of the inflationary process.

The experience of Brazil illustrates the point. The introduction of monetary correction mechanisms in the 1960s created the illusion that living with inflation was not that bad after all, since it was possible to eliminate a great deal of its damaging consequences. As the pace of inflation accelerated, the number of indexation mechanisms increased and prices and contracts became formally adjustable at shorter and shorter time intervals. The period of very high inflation lasted until the mid-1990s. But before managing to put an end to the process, by means of an ingenious monetary reform (the Real Plan), Brazilians were forced to bear the consequences of several (very costly) heterodox plans, involving not only wage and price controls, but the freezing of financial assets as well.

Authors who wrote about the subject in the 1970s and 1980s were not aware of the serious problems caused by indexation as most economists are now. The Brazilian experience certainly contributed to this increased consciousness. Perhaps this can best be illustrated by recalling how common it used to be, at that time, to observe that, to a large extent, the costs of inflation were avoidable consequences of the inflationary process. Robert Shiller, for example, once noticed that the cost associated with price level uncertainty would disappear if the economy were more fully indexed. "We thus do not need to eliminate inflation to deal with this cost", he concluded. (Shiller 1984, p. 52).

In this regard, it is interesting to notice that even Friedman, who always worried about the damaging consequences of inflation, considered indexation a good idea. "The side effects of changes in the rate of inflation can be substantially reduced by encouraging the widespread use of price escalator clauses in private and governmental contracts", he once said. (Friedman 1974, p. 25). He suggested the use of indexation in his own country, while warning that Brazil had adopted it "on a wider scale than I would recommend for the United States". It would be "far better to have no inflation and no escalator clauses. But that alternative [eliminating inflation in the US] is not currently available" (Friedman 1974, p. 35).

Are the costs of moderate inflation small?

The traditional analysis of the costs of inflation led to the conclusion that those costs are small, for moderate rates of inflation. Fischer and Modigliani, for example, started their 1978 paper with the following reasoning: "there is no convincing account of the economic costs of inflation that justifies the typical belief – of the economist and the layman – that inflation poses a serious economic problem, relative to unemployment". (Fischer and Modigliani 1978, p. 810). In the summary made by Shiller in his comments on Fischer's 1984 article, "the standard list of costs of inflation really amounts to nothing much at all, for inflations of moderate range or variability, if the government takes steps to allow indexation". (Shiller 1984, p. 53).

It is interesting to notice that the paper by Fischer and Modigliani was published close to the end of the decade during which, for the first time since World War II, inflation had become a significant phenomenon, in the developed world. In fact, the average rate of inflation (CPI) in the US in 1975-79 was 8.0%. In 1978, the annual rate was 9.0%. In the following year, inflation went up to 13.3% and Paul Volcker was made Fed's chairman.

Volcker's anti-inflationary crusade had already come to an end when the Federal Reserve Bank of Kansas City organized the Jackson Hole symposium around the theme "Price Stability and Public Policy". The year was 1984. Inflation had been brought down from almost 14.0% in 1979 to 3.8% in both 1982 and 1983. At a huge cost – the GDP level observed in the 3Q1982 was practically the same as that in 3Q1979. In spite of the fact that inflation had entered into the double-digit range (becoming number one public enemy) and the tremendous mobilization to bring it down, the tone of the debates, as expressed in Fischer's opinion, was that for those who considered inflation a "deep societal problem" the results of the economic analysis of the costs of inflation – the mirror image of the benefits of price stability – were simply "disappointing". (Fischer, 1984, p. 33).

Inflation and the public opinion

the idea that the costs of inflation are small does not square well with the aversion to inflation reflected in surveys of public opinion. In fact, when the public is surveyed on the issue of inflation, the phenomenon emerges as a social problem of great importance. In the US, prior to the implementation of Volcker's policy, opinion polls indicated it had become the greatest public enemy. But what is it exactly that those surveys generally reveal?

In his 1984 comments, Shiller cited the results of a survey conducted in 1968-70, in the US. Respondents who said their income was higher than it was four years ago were asked to explain why they were now making more. Within the mentioned group, 44 percent said that the income increase was the fruit of their own efforts. They worked hard, acquired more experience and skills, etc. Only 25 percent made reference to external causes, like business conditions or labor unions. And only 6 percent mentioned inflation as the cause of their wage increase. (Shiller 1984, pp. 54-55).

One important result of that survey is that, for the average person, pay raises are not associated with inflation. Respondents apparently believe that they would receive those raises anyway, even in the absence of inflation.

In the mid-1990s, Shiller conducted his own survey. The objective was to understand the reasons why people were apparently so concerned and dismayed by inflation. No doubt, a good understanding of the way the public reacts to the inflationary phenomenon might be quite useful as a guide to economic policy making, helping the government in the process of choosing among different policy options.

Shiller worked with research assistants. They all conducted informal interviews with a randomly chosen sample of people and asked them to answer three different questionnaires. One of them was open-ended (applied only to US respondents) and the others involved multiple choice questions. Besides the US, people in Germany and Brazil were also surveyed. Respondents were classified according to whether they were young or old, economists or non-economists. "Among non-economists in all countries, the largest concern with inflation appears to be that it lowers people's standard of living. Non-economists appear to believe in a sort of sticky-wage model, by which wages do not respond to inflationary shocks, shocks which are themselves perceived as caused by certain people or institutions acting badly". (Shiller 1996, abstract).

The most striking differences between groups were observed between economists and non-economists. In particular, says Shiller, "the general public in the US clearly thinks differently from professional economists about the costs of inflation, far more likely to think of inflation as lowering standards of living". (Shiller 1996, p. 21). The idea is that inflation erodes the purchasing power of wages and therefore eliminates the benefits of justifiable pay raises. Individuals become poorer as a result of inflation.

Understanding what people think are the causes of inflation is of course crucial to the understanding of the reasons for the general belief that inflation hurts people's standards of living. And inflation seems to be attributable to a large number of factors, including greed, big business, (non-specified) government actions, people willing to borrow and spend too much, etc. (Shiller 1996, p. 15). In general, inflation appears to be caused by bad behavior. When prices rise rapidly, people tend to believe that they had been cheated somehow, giving rise to a sense of injustice.

It can be easily seen that the answers differed quite substantially from the list of real effects that Fischer and Modigliani originally offered in their 1978 paper on the costs of inflation. There is little or no mention to the inconveniences created by inflation, to the distortionary effects associated with inflation, to menu costs, etc.

In addition to these findings, the survey conducted by Shiller confirmed the idea that, in general, the public fails to see inflation as a process which tends to affect labor incomes just as it affects the prices of goods and services. "People tend do see the causes of their income increases in personal terms, rather than due to inflation", says the author. (Shiller 1996, p. 16). Such misperception probably explains the significant aversion of wage earners to inflation.

In addition to all this, respondents in the three countries covered by the survey were given two extreme possibilities to choose. One involved a hypothetical very low rate of inflation and a high rate of unemployment. The other involved high inflation and low unemployment. The results indicate that "most people in all countries would choose the low inflation even if it meant that millions more people would be unemployed." (Shiller, 1996, p. 19).

Fischer and Huizinga had come to the same conclusion, as normally happens with anyone who conducts or examines opinion polls on this subject. In a joint paper published in 1982, however, they found an interesting complement. The public generally considers inflation a more serious problem than unemployment, but tends to prefer that economic policy be directed at reducing unemployment, an apparent contradiction deserving further investigation. In the words of the authors, "the results are clearly that the public is in general *not* willing to fight inflation at the cost of higher unemployment – and that is exactly the choice that has been offered by most economists and governments". (Fischer-Huizinga 1982, p. 18).

The monetarist's view

Harry Johnson once examined the social and intellectual conditions which make possible a revolution or counter-revolution in Economics. (Johnson 1971). As had happened with Keynes, the monetarist counter-revolution became a reality only after the appearance of an important economic and social problem which the prevailing orthodoxy could not deal with.

For more than two decades, Friedman had been the leader of a series of research aimed at convincing politicians, economists and the public in general that inflation constituted an important problem and that, contrary to Keynesianism, monetarism explained the phenomenon and had a solution to offer. As emphasized by Johnson, agreement on the second proposition depended on the acceptance of the first one. (Johnson 1971, p. 7). And this only happened as we entered into the 1970s, when the rate of price growth reached a significant level in the United States.

Friedman and his followers dedicated themselves to the study of a subject for which there was no demand in their own country. To obtain an empirical base for their research they concentrated their attention on the inflationary problems of other nations. Demonstrating how things work in practice was a crucial part in the development of the monetarists' ideas. In this regard, the study made by Milton Friedman and Anna Schwartz on the monetary history of the United States was of great importance. Their book examined the evolution of the stock of money in the US during almost 100 years. From this work emerged a large number of empirical relations which helped defining the basic principles of the mentioned school. In particular, the study revealed clear and stable relations between changes in the stock of money, on the one hand, and changes in nominal income, economic activity and prices, on the other. When inflation became a problem, the theoretical framework had already been built.

Friedman's contribution was complemented by his analysis of the Phillips Curve. In a 1967 article (published in the following year), he showed that the trade-off between inflation and unemployment had a temporary nature. In the long run, there was no such trade-off, a conclusion which Edmund Phelps also arrived at, almost simultaneously. As Alan Blinder once put it, "by 1972 the 'vertical-in-the-long-run' view of the Phillips curve had won the day". (Blinder 1992, p. 195).

However, agreement on the inadequacy of exploring the short-run Phillips Curve is not equivalent to recognizing the importance of pursuing low and stable inflation. In fact, years after the idea of the vertical curve had won the day, Friedman's preference for low inflation and for the use of monetary policy was not consensual. (Friedman 1968, p. 13). There was disagreement both in regard to the preferable instrument as well as on how important it was to have low inflation.

Paul Samuelson, Arthur Okun, Walter Heller, James Tobin and several others had opinions quite distant from the ones defended by Friedman. Those economists tended to agree with at least one (if not all of them) of the following statements: a) inflation had its origin in cost pressures; b) incomes policies were highly recommendable; and c) attempts to fight inflation by means of fiscal and monetary restraints would not work. Disagreement in terms of the diagnosis and on the adequate instrument to deal with the inflationary phenomenon was thus quite clear. As to the question regarding how desirable low inflation is, perhaps it suffices to recall a famous reasoning expressed by Tobin: "it takes a heap of Harberger triangles to fill an Okun gap". (Tobin 1977, p. 17).

Central bankers and price stability

On the issue of price stability, academic economists took the backseat. Central bankers took the lead. In the United States, the rate of price growth started to move upwards in the first years of the 1970s. Until then inflation was not a significant phenomenon. Measured by the CPI, the average inflation rate during the preceding decade was 2.3% per annum. For the period 1971-74, inflation figures were distorted by the fact that the initial governmental response to the inflationary problem was the introduction of a program of wage and price controls. Between 1975 and 1979 the price level rose annually at the pace of 8.0%, on average.

As already emphasized, and with the exception of the monetarists, at that time economists were not particularly concerned with the costs to the economy associated with substantial inflation. In the US, as regards the defense of (and the search for) price stability, the lead was taken by policymakers. They were the ones who set the intellectual trend, the first ones to call attention for the importance of low and stable inflation and inflation expectations.

The US experience is obviously quite relevant. But it is important to register that the real pioneers as regards the search for price stability were German and Swiss policymakers. In fact, in the early 1970s, monetary authorities in Germany and Switzerland were long convinced of the need to pursue monetary policies compatible with inflation rates lower than the ones they observed at the time. In Germany, the rate of price growth varied between 5.0% and 7.0% per year. In Switzerland it was even higher. In both countries the dominant influence of money on prices was something already largely recognized. They also understood that in order to obtain lower rates of inflation, monetary policy had to be conducted in an independent way. And that was not possible under the old order represented by the Bretton Woods system of fixed but adjustable exchange rates. Priority was given by individual countries to the stability of the foreign prices of their currencies and this implied lack of control by the monetary authorities over the domestic money supplies. This was particularly true for the two above-mentioned economies.

In the early 1970s, US monetary policy was loose. The economy was weak and experienced external deficits. In a way, the US was exporting inflation to other countries. Germany and Switzerland suffered the most because their currencies were the best candidates to appreciate in any realignment of rates or in case the Bretton Woods system broke down. To defend their currencies, the Germans and the Swiss were forced to acquire enormous amounts of dollars in the international markets. Capital flows were too huge to be fully sterilized, which implied high rates of monetary expansion. This is what produced the relatively high rates of inflation in those economies.

With the collapse of the Bretton Woods system in the first months of 1973, the Germans and the Swiss were free to pursue independent monetary policies. The flexible exchange-rate regime which accompanied that collapse led them to start aiming at lower rates of inflation.

The strategies adopted in both cases were quite similar. Both countries formally introduced monetary targeting, as they established numerical objectives for the expansion of the money supply, whose parameters were set based on informal targets for the inflation rates and were determined by means of the so-called quantity equation. The basic lesson taught by

Milton Friedman and his followers was fully absorbed: inflation was a monetary phenomenon and the task of promoting price stability would be best executed if the central bank opted for targeting a variable under its direct control (the money supply). The objectives were pursued in a non-rigid way and the common strategy was frequently referred to as "pragmatic monetarism", an expression later to be used in the US, during the Volcker administration.

The final results of those two experiences are generally considered to be quite good. In both countries, the average inflation rate converged to less than 2.0% per annum, and stayed at that level for many years. In Germany, the results were particularly good from 1983 onward. From that year until 1990 the average rate of price growth was 1.8%. From 1994 until the creation of the euro, the average rate was 1.6%. This pattern was altered during the period 1991-93 due to the difficulties caused by the German reunification. In Switzerland, something very close to price stability was enjoyed since the mid-1970s. For 25 years, that is, until 1999, when monetary targeting was abandoned, the average inflation rate was 2.7%. From 2000 to 2008 it was only 1.0%.

Back to the US experience, the first thing to recall is that the high rates of price growth observed during the 1970s – especially in the second half of the decade – had transformed inflation into the number one public enemy. This fact clearly created an environment which somehow facilitated a certain change in policymakers' attitude towards inflation.

In mid-1979, the inflation rate was in the double-digit range. In international markets, the dollar had already weakened substantially. Commodity prices were at very high levels, particularly gold. Apparently, there was little confidence in fiat money. There would be elections in the next year. Something had to be done.

At that time, the Fed's chairman was a former executive of an aircraft manufacturer, poorly qualified for the function. Under an atmosphere of crisis, William Miller was given the command of the Treasury, leaving vacant the chairman's position at the Fed. Paul Volcker's experience as a government official, particularly as president of the New York Fed, led several people to suggest his name to President Carter, who (rather reluctantly) accepted the indication.

But before accounting for Volcker's ideas on what needed to be done, and what he actually did after taking the command of the Fed, let us register the then prevailing view regarding anti-inflationary policies in general. In a lecture delivered a few days before Volcker dramatically changed the course of events, Arthur Burns gave a fair picture of that view. Burns was a distinguished academic and had left the Fed's chairmanship the year before, after eight years in the post (1970-78).

The lecture was dubbed "The Anguish of Central Banking" and the question under discussion was the acceleration of inflation in the US. From price stability in the end of the 1950s and early 1960s the country headed for double-digit inflation rates. Burns attributed the persistent inflationary phenomenon to "the philosophic and political currents" that had transformed economic life in the US and elsewhere since the 1930s. He had in mind the activist policies initiated during the New Deal, the Employment Act of 1946 (which made the government responsible for "maximum employment") and the multiplication of governmental programs. (Burns 1979, pp. 9-10). Behind the creation of any new program, benefiting society at large or some particular group, there was the assumption that monetary policy would accommodate the action. In such an environment, the narrative continues, the Fed was always "testing and probing the limits of its freedom" to put inflation under control. (Burns 1979, pp. 15-16). In the end, economic policymaking became dominated by fear of immediate unemployment, rather than fear of current or future inflation. (Burns 1979, p. 13). Years later, Stephen Axilrod, an important economist at the Fed, described the prevailing culture of that time as one of "excessive policy caution". (Axilrod 1996, p. 233).

Greenspan and Bernanke had a similar understanding of the prevailing environment when Volcker took power. In his 2007 book, Greenspan put it this way: "there was a widespread feeling in Washington that since you couldn't bring down inflation without causing more unemployment, it wasn't worth the cost". (Greenspan 2007, p. 83). Bernanke emphasized the absence of "appetite for taking the actions necessary to reduce inflation". (Bernanke 2006, p. 7). Before them, Milton Friedman had already argued that the commitment of the government to a policy of full employment had led the authorities to "overreact to temporary recessions by measures leading to rapid monetary growth". (Friedman 1974, p. 28).

As president of the Federal Reserve Bank of New York, Volcker was a permanent member of the Federal Open Market Committee (Fomc). And as such he had been pressing the Committee for tougher measures against inflation. The transcripts of several Fomc meetings leave this very clear. In one of those meetings, for example, he stressed how impressed he was by the degree that inflation was built into the thinking of businessmen. (Senna 2010, pp. 314-317). He took power as chairman in August 1979, when the annual rate of price growth was around 12.0%.

Within the Fed, the idea of changing the operational procedures of the institution had been a subject under discussion for quite some time. Volcker thought that the right timing for moving from interest-rate targeting to money-supply targeting was finally arriving. In his view, the appropriate moment for that had to coincide with concrete signs of public support for drastic measures against inflation.

In the Fomc extraordinary meeting held on October 6, Volcker stressed the significant worsening of inflationary expectations and submitted the proposal involving regime change to the Committee. He added that there was need for a consensual decision and for a "program that is strong in fact and perceived as strong in terms of dealing with the situation". (Senna 2010, p. 217).

The proposal was approved and the Fed's money desk was given the task of aiming at certain targets for the expansion of the non-borrowed reserves (the main component of the monetary base) of the banking system. The basic interest rate would fluctuate according to the circumstances. In the first three years of the 1980s, it oscillated between 8.0% and 22.0%.

Employment and economic activity suffered as a result of the tightening in monetary policy. The cost of the program was high. The unemployment rate jumped up from an average of 6.0% in 1978-79 to almost 10.0% in 1982-83. Just prior to completing three years, the program was discontinued and there would be no more monetary targeting for the remaining of 1982. At the end of that year inflation was down to 3.8%.

The pressure for interrupting the Fed's strategy at an earlier point was enormous. President Carter lost the run for reelection. Farmers demonstrated by taking their tractors to the streets of Washington and car dealers sent Volcker mailbags full of ignition keys of automobiles they were unable sell. In Kentucky, posters were made in which Volcker and the six other Federal Reserve governors appeared as "wanted". (Treaster 2004, pp. 5-6). In Congress, some members talked about impeaching Volcker, while others considered removing the Fed's power to control the money supply. (Neikirk 1987, p. 128).

To a large extent, success in bringing down the rate of inflation may be attributed to the following reasons: a) the anti-inflationary policy was implemented when inflation was viewed as number one public enemy; b) the supply-side economics which prevailed during the Reagan administration produced huge fiscal deficits, allowing Volcker to shift to the fiscal situation the responsibility for the observed fluctuations in interest rates and the economy; c) Volcker's determination to complete his task was amazing. To illustrate this last point, it suffices to recall that in a testimony before the Committee on Banking, Finance and Urban Affairs, held in mid-1981, when the costs of his program were already high and clear, Volcker calmly said (in the words of one of his biographers) that "almost certainly business failures would multiply and millions more would lose their jobs". (Treaster 2004, p. 4).

The important point to notice is that Volcker did not have a formal academic model in his mind. And he did not follow the thinking of any particular economist. The Keynesian idea of the need to create an output gap to be able to bring inflation down, for example, did not make part of his reasoning. From the monetarist school, he kept only its fundamental principle: inflation is a monetary phenomenon. Perhaps just as important for the accomplishment of his task (and for future monetary developments) was his emphasis on the role of low and stable inflationary expectations. In an article published three years before ascending to the chairmanship, he made that clear. He rejected Friedman's idea of adopting a constant rate of growth for the money supply. No central banker, he said, would be willing to dispose of some sort of hedge against uncertainty, which is equivalent to saying that it is wise to preserve certain flexibility to be able to face unpredictable events, to test new measures, and to examine market reactions and benefit from them. At that occasion, he made use of the expression "pragmatic monetarism". (pp. 251-52).

While academic economists were arguing that the costs of inflation were small, in Europe and in the US policy makers were fighting to reduce the rate of price growth. In Europe, the economic turbulences which marked the end of the Bretton Woods system caused a revival of the idea of building a monetary union. As a first step in this direction, several European countries embarked into a regime called the European Monetary System (EMS). One important component of that scheme was the Exchange-Rate Mechanism (ERM), according to which the countries that opted to participate would fix the external price of their currencies to the Deutsch mark. The exchange rates were adjustable, in accordance with some principles. Those countries which decided to take part were attempting to import the German monetary-authority credibility. The mechanism was in place from 1979 until 1993. Disinflation was substantial. The results were summarized by Paul De Grauwe. "From a peak of 11% in 1980, the rate of inflation within the system declined to an average of 2% in 1988. During the early 1990s it hovered around 3%". (De Grauwe 1994, p. 133).

Volcker was replaced by Alan Greenspan, whose administration continued to work toward stabilizing inflation and inflation expectations. In the first few years of the Greenspan period, inflation rose again. But taking advantage of the weakness of the economy in the beginning of the 1990s, the Fed managed to bring inflation down, substantially. From 1991 until 2005 (Greenspan left at the end of January 2006), the average rate of inflation was 2.6% per annum. In the words of Ben Bernanke, "like Volcker, Greenspan was ahead of academic thinking in recognizing the potential benefits of increased price stability". (Bernanke 2006, p. 9).

The early 1990s marked the appearance of a new monetary policy strategy. In the first four years of the decade New Zealand, Canada, the United Kingdom and Sweden became pioneers in the adoption of inflation targeting (IT). They were followed by a series of other countries. In all those economies the authorities were already convinced of the importance of price stability as a macroeconomic goal. As policy makers moved toward the adoption of IT, it became necessary to give a numerical interpretation to the concept of price stability. The relevant question then was: what particular inflation rate should be targeted?

Some of the IT adopters considered it unwise to head immediately to their preferable long-run target. And while some chose to pursue the conventional headline inflation, other opted for aiming at some measure of underlying inflation. Independently from the revealed preference, the general choice was for a target between 1.0% and 3.0% per annum. (Bernanke-Laubach-Mishkin-Posen 1999).

The early years of the 1990s also saw concrete signs of increasing acceptance by the academic world of the idea of price stability as an important long-run goal. The 1996 traditional symposium sponsored by the Federal Reserve Bank of Kansas City, held in Jackson Hole, was organized under the title "Achieving Price Stability". Stanley Fischer was there and gave one of the key speeches, dubbed "Why Are Central Banks Pursuing Long-Run Price Stability?". The change in tone was clear. In his words, "the fundamental reason to pursue long-run price stability is that – as has long been argued by central bankers and is increasingly accepted by academic economists – inflation is economically and socially costly". (Fischer 1996, p. 8). This statement is essentially different from arguing that the costs of moderate inflation are not only small but can be largely mitigated by indexation. Furthermore, the statement acknowledges the leading role played by central bankers on the issue of price stability and represents an explicit recognition of the fact that academics adapted their views on the subject.

Fischer discussed a list of factors which influenced his idea of "the optimal rate of inflation". And concluded that the "arguments point to a target inflation rate in the 1 to 3 percent range; more specifically, they suggest that inflation should be targeted at about 2 percent, to stay within a range of 1 to 3 percent per year". Since inflation is not totally controllable, it seemed wise to specify a range. (Fischer 1996, pp. 18-20).

Also present at the symposium, Lawrence Summers expressed this opinion: "I think it is clear that high rates of inflation, by which I mean rates that exceed 4 or 5 percent, have obvious costs that outweigh any possible benefits". (Summers 1996, p. 36). Academic opinion on the costs of inflation had really changed.

The case of Brazil

In June 2004, headed by the Brazilian Finance Minister, the National Monetary Council defined an inflation target of 4.5%, with a tolerance margin of 2.0% in both directions, for the year 2006. These parameters have been kept constant since then. For 2005, the target had already been established at 4.5%, but the margin was half of a percentage point larger in both directions. Since that year, measured by the change in the IPCA, for seven times the observed rate of inflation in Brazil stayed above the 4.5% objective and only three times below it. In the last four years, the average rate of inflation was 6.04%, the lowest rate being 5.84%. Inflationary expectations have adjusted accordingly. As of this writing, information collected by the Central Bank of Brazil, in a survey presently covering around 100 institutions, indicate that the expected average price level change is 6.2% for the coming 12-month period. This means that we are far from having price stability.

The way inflation has recently been dealt with in Brazil probably imposes significant costs to our society. To begin with, we must call attention for an image cost, associated with the fact that governments which show difficulties to control inflation tend to be seen as governments which lack the resources and willingness to have other areas of the economy under adequate control as well.

A second component of the costs has to do with the country's tax system. In the past, the years of high inflation forced the system to undergo profound adaptations. Sophisticated mechanisms were introduced with the objective of eliminating (or mitigating) distortions caused by the high rates of price growth. Since the monetary reform of 1994, though, the legislation does not contemplate the possibility of formal monetary-correction devices. This is particularly troublesome as regards firms' balance sheets. Depreciation allowance does not apply to the adjusted values of fixed assets and there is no room for correcting firms' capital bases. Nominal profits are being taxed.

In regard to individual income tax, there are two questions. One relates to transactions in the secondary real-estate market. The difference between the sale price and the acquisition price is taxed at the rate of 15%, with no room for monetary correction of the historical price. The seller may be exempt in case he acquires another property in the same municipality, within six months, but the law clearly hurts the functioning of the market and invites tax evasion. The other point relates to nominal income brackets, which in recent years have been corrected by projected (underestimated) inflation, rather than by observed inflation. As noted above, the government benefits by not indexing the tax system and tends to resist pressures to make the adequate adjustments.

While there may be reasons for not attributing much importance to the so-called shoe-leather and menu costs, the same does not apply to the uncertainty and allocative problems derived from inflation. As discussed earlier, economists do not agree on how harmful to economic growth moderate rates of inflation are. Nevertheless, the fact that it is difficult to evaluate the impact of a given phenomenon (inflation) on the behavior of a certain macroeconomic variable (GDP growth) does not necessarily mean that the effect does not exist. In our opinion, the hypothesis that inflation hurts economic growth is a good one to work with.

After the disinflation period observed in Brazil in the beginning of the 2000s, inflation has shown a new rising tendency, especially if we concentrate our attention on the behavior of the so-called free prices, representing approximately 77% of the official inflation index (IPCA). This subset of the IPCA stayed below 3.5% per annum between November 2006 and July 2007, excluding food prices. If we observe the behavior of this indicator since that time until the present days, we notice that the monthly average rate went up from 5.2% in 2007-09 to 6.6% in 2010-13, in annual terms. At the same time the variance rose from 4.7 to 8.5.

This finding represents additional evidence of the idea that the higher the rate of price growth, the higher its variability. Its policy implication seems clear. If we want to have lower rates of interest in Brazil (apparently a national demand) we need to have lower inflation and inflation expectations. Under the present monetary policy framework, these require lower (credible) target rates. Otherwise, nominal and real interest rates will continue to incorporate higher inflation expectations and considerable risk premiums, associated with the uncertainty regarding inflation in the future.

Considering the possible unwillingness on the part of the public to bear the costs of anti-inflationary programs – a conclusion based on opinion surveys conducted in the US and which demands broader investigation – as a general guideline, it seems wise to maintain inflation rates as low as possible, so that it will not be necessary to reduce it at a later point. In principle, the higher the level reached by inflation, the more unstable it becomes and the higher the costs of combatting it.

Thus, for several reasons, it seems really desirable to reduce inflation in Brazil, a decision that would involve setting a new target for the inflation rate. But how low this new level should be?

The main arguments for aiming at some positive rate of price growth are well known. First, price indexes in general do not consider changes in the quality of goods and services. Furthermore, price indexes of the fixed-weight type, like the IPCA, do not take into account the fact that consumers usually diminish the purchases of items whose prices go up and go for their substitutes. There is a tendency, then, for the index to overstate the "true" rate of inflation. Depending on the magnitude of the bias, a positive but very low rate of inflation may in fact represent deflation, an undesirable event.

Second, to the extent that nominal wages present downward rigidity, reductions in real wages (sometimes necessary to avoid increased unemployment) can occur only through inflation. The fact that the Brazilian legislation prohibits reductions in nominal wages makes this point even more relevant, the conclusion being that in the case of Brazil it is particularly important not to aim at too low inflation.

Third, if inflation is set at too low a level, the policy rate of interest, in nominal terms, will be too low as well, thus reducing the leeway that central banks usually need to accommodate their strategy in the presence (or threat) of a weakened economy.

Taking all these factors into consideration, we would suggest that the long-run target be established at 3.0% per annum, with a tolerance margin of 1.0% in both directions. Since it would be too unrealistic, or too costly, to make this change in a single jump, we propose a gradual approach. As a first step, this would require getting back to the 4.5% objective, making sure that inflation expectations have really converged to that level, with no signs of price repression.

References

Axilrod, Stephen, 1996, "General Discussion", Achieving Price Stability, A Symposium Sponsored by the Federal Reserve Bank of Kansas City, Jackson Hole, Wyoming, August, 29-31.

Bailey, Martin, 1956, "The Welfare Cost of Inflationary Finance". *The Journal of Political Economy*, vol. LXIV, April, number 2.

Bernanke, Ben S., 2006, "The Benefits of Price Stability", The Federal Reserve Board, Speech delivered at the Center for Economic Policy Studies, Princeton University, Princeton, New Jersey, February 24.

Bernanke, Ben S., Thomas Laubach, Frederic S. Mishkin and Adam S. Posen, 1999, *Inflation Targeting – Lessons from the International Experience*. Princeton: Princeton University Press.

Blinder, Alan S., 1992, "Commentary: Déjà Vu All Over Again", in *The Business Cycle: Theories and Evidence*, ed. by Michael T. Belongia and Michele R. Garfinkel. Boston: Kluwer Academic Publishers.

Burns, Arthur F., 1979, "The Anguish of Central Banking", *The 1979 Per Jacobsson Lecture*. Washington. D.C.: Per Jacobsson Foundation, September.

De Grauwe, Paul, 1994, *The Economics of Monetary Integration*. Oxford: Oxford University Press.

Fischer, Stanley, 1981, "Towards an Understanding of the Costs of Inflation: II", Carnegie-Rochester Conference Series on Public Policy 15, The Costs and Consequences of Inflation.

Fischer, Stanley, 1984, "The Benefits of Price Stability", in Price Stability and Public Policy, A Symposium Sponsored by the Federal Reserve Bank of Kansas City, Jackson Hole, Wyoming, August 2-3.

Fischer, Stanley, 1996, "Why Are Central Banks Pursuing Long-Run Price Stability?", Achieving Price Stability, A Symposium Sponsored by the Federal Reserve Bank of Kansas City, Jackson Hole, Wyoming, August 29-31.

Fischer, Stanley and Franco Modigliani, 1978, "Towards an Understanding of the Real Effects and Costs of Inflation", Weltwirtschaftliches Arquiv, 114.

Fischer, Stanley and John Huizinga, 1982, "Inflation, Unemployment, and Public Opinion Polls", Journal of Money, Credit and Banking, vol. 14, no. 1, February.

Fisher, Irving, [1911] 1963, *The Purchasing Power of Money – Its Determination and Relation to Credit, Interest and Crises*. New York: Augustus M. Kelley.

Friedman, Milton, 1974, "Monetary Correction", in *Essays on Inflation and Indexation*. Washington. D. C., American Enterprise Institute for Public Policy Research.

Friedman, Milton, 1968, "The Role of Monetary Policy", *The American Economic Review*, vol. LVIII, no. 1, March.

Greenspan, Alan, 2007, *The Age of Turbulence – Adventures in a New World*. New York: The Penguin Press.

Johnson, Harry G., 1971, "The Keynesian Revolution and the Monetarist Counter-Revolution", *The American Economic Review*, vol. 61, no. 2, May.

Keynes, John M., [1923] 2000, *A Track on Monetary Reform*. New York: Prometheus Books.

Keynes, John M. [1931] 1963, *Essays in Persuasion*. New York: W. W. Norton.

Neikirk, William R., 1987, *Volcker: Portrait of the Money Man*. New York: Congdon & Weed.

Phillips, A. W., 1958, "The Relation between Unemployment and the Rate of Change of Money Wage Rates in the United Kingdom, 1861-1957", *Economica*, vol. 25, November.

Samuelson, Paul A. and Robert M. Solow, 1960, "Analytical Aspects of Anti-Inflation Policy", *The American Economic Review*, v. 50, n.2, May.

Senna, José Júlio, 2010, *Política Monetária: Ideias, Experiências e Evolução*. Rio de Janeiro: Editora FGV.

Shiller, Robert J., 1984, "Commentary", Price Stability and Public Policy, A Symposium Sponsored by the Federal Reserve Bank of Kansas City, Jackson Hole, Wyoming, August 2-3.

Shiller, Robert J., 1996, "Why Do People Dislike Inflation?", NBER Working Paper no. 5539, National Bureau of Economic Research.

Summers, Lawrence, 1996, "Commentary: Why Are Central Banks Pursuing Long-Run Price Stability?", Achieving Price Stability, A Symposium Sponsored by the Federal Reserve Bank of Kansas City, Jackson Hole, Wyoming, August 29-31.

Tobin, James, 1977, "How Dead is Keynes?", Cowles Foundation Discussion Paper No. 458, July 12.

Treaster, Joseph B., 2004, *Paul Volcker – The Making of a Financial Legend*. Hoboken, New Jersey: John Wiley & Sons.

4

On "secular stagnation" and the equilibrium real interest rate

The original idea

In 1938, Harvard Professor Alvin Hansen, at that time the leading Keynesian economist in America, was elected president of the American Economic Association. The presidential address, entitled "Economic Progress and Declining Population Growth", was delivered on December 28 of that year. At the occasion, he made use of the expression "secular stagnation".

Hansen, probably influenced by the length and severity of the Great Depression, was concerned with the possibility that the era of growth and prosperity which had characterized the Western world after the Industrial Revolution might be coming to an end. Later, as the US entered into World War II, economic activity intensified. But the big question was what would happen in the future, when the conflict ended. In the opinion of many, economic growth was threatened by the possibility of lack of investment demand.

Modern economic textbooks do not mention Hansen's once famous expression. It fell out of use, as his concern proved to be unfounded. Contrary to what many imagined, the immediate post-war years were marked by rapid rates of economic growth and low rates of unemployment, a picture which did not change much for a couple of decades. The baby boom modified the trend in population growth and productivity gains were high until the early 1970s.

More recently, the slow pace of the recovery from the 2008 financial crisis, and some aspects of the behavior of the American economy in the years prior to the crisis, led Lawrence Summers to revive the "secular stagnation" idea.

A brief look at the views put forward by Hansen in the final years of the 1930s allows one to compare the discussion which arose in the wake of the remarks made by Summers with the one which came up seven and a half decades ago.

What had made possible the great rise in the standard of living of Western Europe and the United States since the beginning of the Industrial Revolution was the rapid growth of capital formation during that period, says Hansen. And the "external forces" (as he called them) behind that process were: a) inventions; b) the discovery and development of new territory and new resources; and c) the growth of population. (Hansen 1939, pp. 3-4). In his conjectures, he concluded that "the opening of new territory and the growth of population were together responsible for a very large fraction – possibly somewhere near one-half – of the total volume of new capital formation in the nineteenth century". (Hansen 1939, p. 9). The then projected decline in population growth and the lack of important areas left for exploitation and settlement meant that those two outlets for new investments were being closed.

Declining population growth would affect the pace of capital accumulation especially through a diminished demand for residential housing. And there would be a negative impact on the rate of investments in public utilities and in the manufacture of essential consumers' goods as well. Additionally, Hansen argued that there would be no basis for assuming that one could count on the emergence of new industries as rich in investment opportunities as the railroad or, more recently, the automobile, with all the related developments, public roads in particular. He concluded that "when a revolutionary new industry like the railroad or the automobile, after having initiated in its youth a powerful upward surge of investment activity, reaches maturity and ceases to grow, as all industries must, the whole economy must experience a profound stagnation, unless indeed new developments take its place". (Hansen 1939, p. 10).

The revival of the hypothesis

The idea of secular stagnation was revived in a speech delivered by Summers at an IMF Economic Forum held in November 2013. Referring to the years prior to the crisis, Summers recalled that the US economy had experienced a couple of bubbles, in housing and the stock market. At the same time, lending by the banking industry was increasing at fast rates, the same being true as regards private sector debt. According to his reasoning, such an environment should have led to an overheated economy, that is, high rates of output growth and inflation. But this was not what happened.

Some statistics might be useful to illustrate the argument. Between 2002 and 2007, measured by the Case-Shiller 10 index, the cumulative rise in the average price of housing was 62%. If we consider the 1998-2005 period, that index went up by 166%. In the stock market, the S&P 500 index increased cumulatively by almost 30%, and was particularly strong between 2003 and 2006 (a cumulative rise by almost 60%). In the banking industry, the total volume of loans and leases went up by 74%. The other side of this coin was a considerable increase in the size of debt in the private sector, reinforcing a tendency which had started years before. If we look only at household debt, it represented roughly 75% of GDP in the beginning of 2002 and it went up to practically 100% in the end of 2007, while the corresponding ratio in the middle of 1980s was less than 50%. On the monetary side, the average real rate of interest was 0.3% per year (the policy rate corrected for the PCE), down from 2.8% in the 1990s.

The numbers above seem to justify the summary made by Summers: "too easy money, too much borrowing, too much wealth". (Summers 2013). But in spite of all these stimuli, the GDP growth rate was 2.7% on average and inflation was 2.5% (averages for 2002-07), numbers which are far from extraordinary.

Summers would soon elaborate a bit more on his original reasoning. And he made clear that he was talking about the developed world, and not only the US. Referring to the Eurozone, for example, he observed that the good performance of the region in its first ten years of existence was not sustainable and was dependent on financial flows to the periphery, which, viewed in retrospect, characterized a bubble. As he put it, the record of the industrial world "over the last 15 years is profoundly discouraging as to the prospect of maintaining substantial growth with financial stability". (Summers 2014a, p. 69).

Perhaps the most striking fact which accompanied the creation of the euro was the convergence of long-term interest rates. As we approached 1999, when the monetary union was to become a reality, the long-term rates on government bonds in general got closer and closer to the rates paid by the bonds issued by Germany, the largest and soundest economy in the region. With the launching of the single currency, those rates became practically the same, a situation which lasted until the second half of 2008. This happened even in the case of Greece, which joined the euro two years after its creation.

The fact that the monetary policy rate was set at a rather low level, and considering that inflation rates varied from country to country, meant that there were periods of negative rates, especially in some peripheral economies. On average, the real policy rate was 0.4% per annum, between 2002 and 2007. Long-term rates were low during the mentioned period.

Particularly in peripheral countries, increased confidence and favorable financial conditions set the stage for a tremendous increase in borrowing activity. In a short paper published in 2010, Paul De Grauwe showed that, as a proportion of GDP, household debt in the Eurozone went up from a little over 50% in 1999 to 56% in 2002 and almost 70% in 2007. Bank liabilities in the Eurozone also increased substantially, especially in the 2002-07 period. As a proportion of GDP they went up from 190% to around 250%. (De Grauwe 2010, pp.2-3). Practically absent in Italy, the burst of optimism was particularly intense in Spain and Ireland, where the borrowing spree produced housing bubbles.

On the lending side, the stock of credit provided by the banking industry increased by 56% between 2002 and 2007. Banks certainly felt encouraged not only by the prevailing favorable climate but also by the disappearance of the exchange-rate risk. Those which had been reluctant to lend money in the currencies of countries in the region's periphery suddenly became quite willing to do so in euros.

As in the case of the US economy, one might expect that such extraordinarily positive environment would have produced abnormal rates of economic growth and possibly a rising inflationary tendency. But this was not what we saw. In the 2002-2007 period, economic growth averaged 2.0% per annum and inflation averaged 2.2%. The corresponding figures for the peripheral countries (the so-called PIIGS) were a bit higher than those numbers, respectively, 2.9% and 3.0%.

The experience of industrial countries in the years which preceded the crisis led Summers to wonder whether those economies needed bubbles to achieve reasonable rates of economic growth. Apparently, in the absence of those bubbles, growth would have been anemic, due to lack of effective demand.

In his efforts to understand what might explain the situation prevailing before the crisis, Summers discusses the possibility that structural changes (involving shifts in savings and investment) could have caused a decline in the equilibrium real rate of interest. In this case, lower levels of observed real (and nominal) interest rates would be a major factor stimulating borrowing and risk-seeking investors. Such a hypothesis seems compatible with the macroeconomic experience of those years.

Summers examines several changes which might have produced a substantial fall in the short-term real interest rate that is consistent with full employment. In reality, he even considers the possibility that "no attainable interest rate will permit the balancing of saving and investment at full employment, [which] is the secular stagnation hypothesis first put forward by Alvin Hansen in the 1930s". (Summers 2014b, p. 32).

The major possible changes would be: a) an increase in savings (a decline in the propensity to spend) as a result of changes in the distribution of income, which favored capital as opposed to labor income, and benefitted individuals with more wealth as opposed to those with less; b) a diminished demand for capital goods due to slower population growth; c) a contraction in the demand for debt-financed investment associated with a new structure of the productive economy – "it used to require tens of millions of dollars to start a significant new venture, and significant new ventures today are seeded with hundreds of thousands of dollars" (Summers 2014a, p. 69); d) a substantial decline in the relative price of business equipment, which implies less borrowing and spending. All of them probably contributed to drive down the interest rates on safe assets.

Perhaps the simplest way to illustrate the essence of the discussion involves recourse to an old analytical instrument: the IS schedule. In graph 1 the equilibrium real rate of interest results from the interaction between the IS curve and the level of real potential output. In the context of the present discussion, it was first used by Paul Krugman a couple of months before the now famous speech made by Summers. (Krugman 2013). Krugman was already concerned with the old idea of stagnation associated with persistently inadequate aggregate demand.

Under normal conditions, forces in the economy would generate an equilibrium real rate given by r1 in the graph. The central bank supposedly manipulates its policy rate with the objective of taking it to that level, where the output gap is zero, that is, economic activity is at its potential. Such is the level compatible with stable inflation. Assume now that structural changes in the economy give rise to shifts in savings and investment of the kinds suggested by those concerned with the stagnation hypothesis. Both an increase in savings as well as a contraction in investment causes the IS schedule to shift downward. The equilibrium rate of interest falls. It may even become negative, as indicated by r2 in the graph.

The downward shift of the IS curve means that aggregate demand declined. Assuming that monetary authorities normally guide themselves by an estimate of the equilibrium real rate of interest, as they suspect of a falling rate they lower the policy rate, in a movement whose intensity depends on their objective function, or legal mandate.

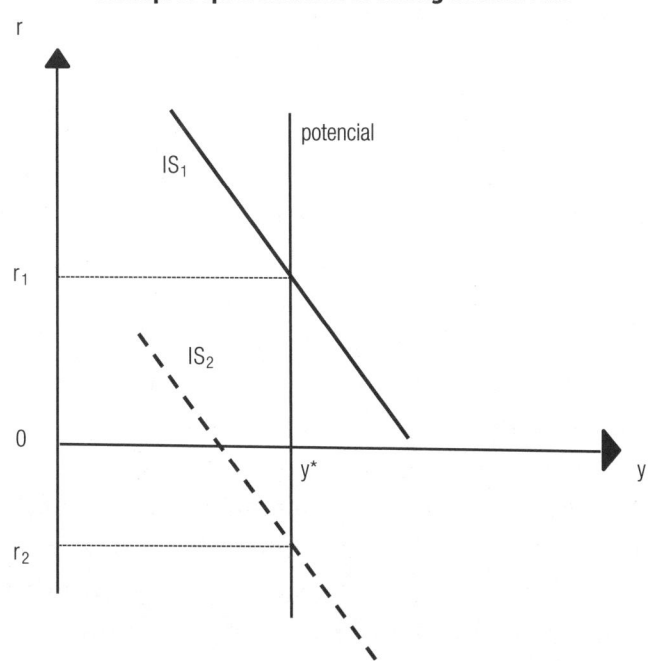

Graph 1
A simple representation of falling neutral rate

Within this framework of analysis, the lowering of the real policy rates in industrial countries in the years prior to the crisis were normal responses to the perception (by the authorities) of declining equilibrium real rates. This action of the central banks stimulated the forces already at work in the direction of more borrowing and leverage.

In general, in their analyses of the equilibrium real rate of interest, what economists have in mind is the real return on short-term assets considered to be safe, as US Treasury bills, for example. In spite of the fact that the Hansen-Summers theoretical framework is designed for a closed economy, Summers seems to be aware of the influence of external factors on the determination of the basic interest rate in the US, since he recognizes, for example, that the "rising desire of central banks and governments to accumulate reserves, coupled with conservative investment strategies operates to raise the demand for safe assets". (Summers 2014b, p. 34). In reality, in a financially-integrated world as the one we have now, that specific interest rate is not determined exclusively by forces within the US. In this case, it depends on the global supply of funds, the global demand for funds and the relative demand for safe assets.

A recent IMF study published as chapter 3 of the April 2014 World Economic Outlook discusses the declining movement of equilibrium real interest rate in recent times from a global perspective. The study shows that the degree of financial integration increased steadily since the 1980s. In consequence, the dispersion of interest rates among different countries diminished considerably. This would be an evidence of the growing influence of common factors in the determination of interest rates, allowing us to speak of global interest rates.

Before examining the way (and the reasons why) those rates moved in recent times, let us recall that the equilibrium real rate of interest is a variable that cannot be observed. Frequently, it is also referred to as the neutral or natural rate. In general, central bankers conduct monetary policy with an eye on what they believe the equilibrium rate is. When inflation rates are above the desired level, and the authorities wish to bring them back to that level, the real policy rate has to be set at a level higher than the neutral one. If the economy is weak and the authorities wish to stimulate it, the real policy rate needs to be set at a level below the neutral. Since any economy is constantly subject to the influence of cyclical forces, the observed real policy rate rarely corresponds to the rate that the central bank believes to be the neutral one.

Assuming for a moment that we can identify the equilibrium real rate for a number of countries, which factors would make them differ? In an economy financially isolated from the rest of the world, no external force is capable of influencing her neutral rate. In this case, the rate is totally determined by the interaction of domestic savings and domestic investment. Thus, the degree of financial openness is part of the answer. The other factor is credit risk. Government securities issued by different countries are normally perceived as commanding different risk premiums. A higher perceived risk implies a higher neutral rate. In sum, rates across countries tend to differ according to their degree of financial integration and to specific factors associated with credit risk.

If the world were made only of countries that would issue government securities perceived to be risk free, and were totally integrated from the financial viewpoint, arbitrage transactions would guarantee the uniqueness of the neutral real rate.

Over short time horizons, short-term and long-term interest rates may move in different directions. However, over the medium and long run, they tend to move together. The above-mentioned IMF study shows that the average global rates computed for three months and ten years, for samples of almost 20 countries (weighted by the corresponding GDPs), experienced a clear downward trend since the early 1980s (Graph 2). Both rates fell by approximately six percentage points. The short-term one declined from 4.0% in real terms to minus 2.0%. The long-term one fell from 6.0% to practically zero. (IMF 2014).

Two distinct phenomena apparently affected the behavior of global real interest rates since the beginning of the 1980s. The first phenomenon had to do with the fact that real rates were considerably high to begin with, as a result of the fact that at that time central banks (particularly in the US) were involved in a tough fight against the inflationary process that had erupted in the 1970s. As the fruits of the anti-inflationary war started to appear, real rates were gradually brought down. In other words, interest rates were abnormally high in the beginning of the 1980s because monetary authorities had set their policy rates well above any reasonable estimates of the neutral levels. In a nutshell, cyclical deviations predominated in the first ten years.

A different phenomenon apparently prevailed in the 2000s. Financial integration increased at a fast rate during that period. And some emerging markets (particularly in Asia) experienced an important structural change, namely, their aggregate savings expanded considerably. This was particularly true in China, where the excess of savings over investment meant an enormous surplus in the current account. On average, it reached 9.3% of GDP in 2006-07. Due to the fact that for the world economy as a whole the balance in the current account is necessarily zero (except for statistical discrepancies), any increase in the surplus of a group of countries necessarily corresponds to an increase in the deficit of another group. As the Chinese were saving more, the Americans, for example, were investing more, in comparison to their domestic saving effort. Current account deficits in the US balance of payments reached 5.3% of GDP in 2006-07.

Graph 2
Short and long-term global real interest rates (in %)

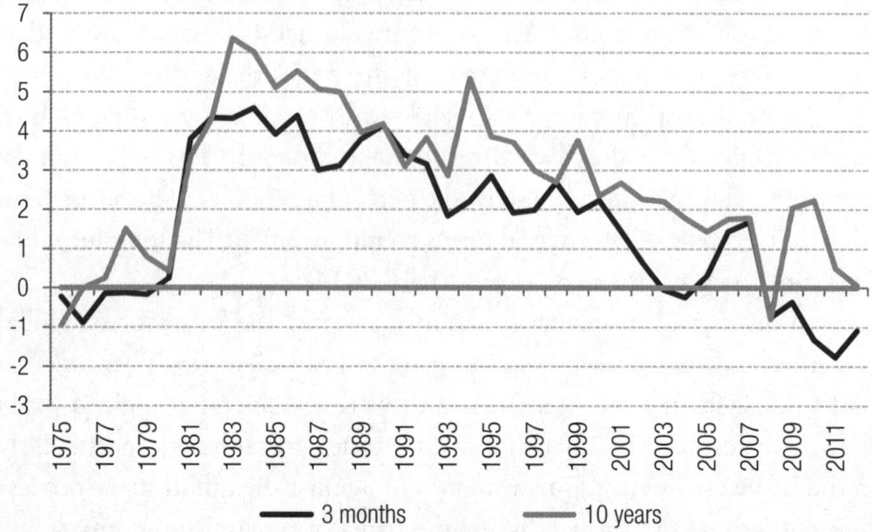

― 3 months   ― 10 years

Average rates weighted by GDPs (18 countries for short-term rates; 19 countries for the long-term rates). Latest information: 2012. Source: IMF, World Economic Outlook, April 2014, Chapter 3.

What this means is that the relevance of shifts in current-account balances can only be evaluated ex-post. And the taste of the pudding lies exactly in observing the movements of real interest rates. To the extent that, in a financially integrated world, the equilibrium real rate of interest is the result of interaction between global savings and investment (with due account taken for the behavior of the relative demand for safe assets), we can say that the dominant movement behind the observed decline in real interest rates during the 2000s was probably an expansion of global savings, a contraction of global investment, or both.

The possibility of a saving glut was first raised in a speech made by Ben Bernanke in 2005. At the occasion, the then governor of the Fed argued that "over the past decade a combination of diverse forces has created a significant increase in the global supply of saving – a global saving glut – which helps to explain both the increase in the U.S. current account deficit and the relatively low level of long-term real interest rates in the world today". (Bernanke 2005, p. 1). In his analysis, he stressed the factors that might explain the transformation of a large number of emerging economies from borrowers to net lenders in international capital markets.

The above-mentioned IMF study reinforced the point made by Bernanke. In fact, the authors concluded that "a steady increase in income growth in emerging market economies during 2000-07 led to substantially higher saving rates in these economies". And this would have been a major factor behind the observed decline in real interest rates during that period. They also concluded that, since the crisis, the dominant force has probably been "a sharp and persistent decline in investment rates in advanced economies". (IMF 2014, p. 1).

In sum, the experience of the industrial world in the years which preceded the crisis was a peculiar one. In spite of so many stimuli those economies did not produce any sign of overheating, neither in terms of economic activity, nor in the inflationary field. Were it not for those stimuli, economic growth would have been anemic.

To the extent that this whole reasoning makes sense, the monetary authorities faced a difficult dilemma. Lowering the policy rates may have stimulated the formation of bubbles and the borrowing spree, but it certainly contributed to the maintenance of the growth process, without significant inflation. Had the central banks refused to follow what seemed to be a declining trend of the equilibrium real rate of interest, they would have hurt the growth process and probably allowed for undesirable deflationary pressures. This is probably the gist of the message sent by Summers. Structural changes made it difficult for industrial economies to achieve full employment, economic growth and financial stability at the same time.

The dilemma becomes even more serious if we are willing to accept the hypothesis that the short-term real interest rate consistent with full employment had fallen into negative territory, as illustrated in graph 1.

To the extent that the equilibrium rate becomes negative, and as long as inflation rates are relatively low, pursuing the neutral level becomes practically impossible, for the simple reason that the nominal rate has a zero lower bound. Since at some point this limit has been reached in important industrial economies (perhaps sometime in the middle of the last decade), one is well advised to give some credit to that hypothesis.

A supply-side approach

Economic stagnation or slow growth persisting over an indefinitely long period is the threat contained in the secular stagnation hypothesis. Interestingly, when the discussion around this issue sprang, Robert Gordon had already expressed his concern with the slowing down of US economic growth.

Strictly speaking, Gordon's contribution is not directly related to the "secular stagnation" hypothesis. While this hypothesis is a demand-related idea, his work has to do with the supply side of the economy. Nevertheless, it became part of the debate for the simple reason that the two approaches have in common the same concern. Notice that the financial crisis plays no role in Gordon's analysis and that he shows no interest on what happens to the equilibrium rate of interest.

Gordon's arguments have given rise to considerable controversy. In a 2012 paper, he claimed that two different factors would contribute to a substantial fall in the rate of growth of the US economy, from 2007 onward. (Gordon 2012). The first one was a set of headwinds. The second one was related to an idea that he had developed several years earlier, involving a comparison of the effects of Industrial Revolution III (computers, the web, mobile phones) and Industrial Revolution II (electricity, internal combustion engine, internal plumbing). Gordon believes that IR#2 was more important and more pervasive than IR#3, with stronger impact on productivity growth. (Gordon 2000).

In a sequel paper Gordon made use of a quite provocative title, in which he spoke of the "demise" of US economic growth. (Gordon 2014). The starting point of the second paper was a simple identity: output per capita equates labor productivity (output divided by hours worked) times hours per capita. The behavior of those variables was observed over a long period (1891-2013), divided into four sub-periods. Hours per capita showed a declining trend and its rate of growth was positive in only one of the sub-periods (1972-1996), as a result (basically) of an increase in female labor force participation. The author's projections indicate hours per capita falling at a rate of minus 0.3% per annum. One of the main factors contributing for this negative growth will be the retirement of the baby boomers.

As to labor productivity, Gordon estimates that the first sub-period (1891-1972) corresponded to the golden age of productivity gains, which averaged 2.4% per annum. The author associates those gains with the great inventions of the last three or four decades of the XIX century (IR#2).

Productivity gains slowed down in the early 1970s (it grew at an annual rate of 1.4% in 1972-96), giving rise to a debate regarding the nature of the slowdown. Was it a temporary or a permanent phenomenon? As we entered the age of widespread use of computers, many analysts imagined that productivity growth was bound to go up again. "You can see the computer age everywhere but in the productivity statistics", noted Robert Solow, in 1987. The results of the computer revolution finally appeared in the data, but they did not last long. Productivity gains were slightly stronger than those of the golden age, but they remained high only in 1996-2004, the most fertile years of IR#3 (average growth of 2.5%). Gordon argues that "the boom of the late 1990s was driven by an unprecedented and never-repeated rate of decline in the price of computer speed and memory, and a never since matched surge in the share of GDP devoted to information and communication technology (ICT) investment." (Gordon 2014, p. 20). After 2004, productivity growth slowed down once again (average of 1.3% in 2004-13).

The short-lived nature of the "New Economy" and Gordon's expectations that nothing extraordinary (in comparison to IR#2) is about to happen in the field of innovations in the foreseeable future (an obviously bold assumption) led him to work with only two sub-periods, as far as the rhythm of productivity gains is concerned. The first corresponds to the golden age (1891-1972) and the second is made of the years between 1972 and 2013. Productivity gains averaged 2.4% in the first one and 1.6% in the second one.

In projecting the growth of GDP per capita for the coming decades, Gordon uses as reference the annual growth rate of GDP per capita between 1891 and 2007. That rate was 2.0%. He projects growth in the 25 or 40 years after 2007 by making adjustments to that number. As already mentioned, from 2.0% per annum we need to subtract 0.3%, the estimated negative influence of hours per capita.

As to productivity, he works with the 1.6% figure referred to above. This is equivalent to saying that he expects no major change in the field of innovations, that is, productivity gains will keep the pace observed since the early 1970s. Given that productivity growth in the reference period (1891-2007) was 2.2% per annum, the adjustment factor is 0.6%. Finally, there is an additional adjustment to the productivity figure, in the magnitude of 0.2%, to account for the fact that educational attainment has stagnated. The author recalls that increased educational attainment (particularly the surge in high-school graduation) was a central driver of 20th century economic growth. (Gordon 2014, p. 10). For Gordon, there are only two sources of labor productivity growth: innovation and improvements in labor quality through increased educational attainment. "Capital deepening and changes in capital quality are endogenous to innovation", he says. (Gordon 2014, p. 22).

Performing the necessary subtractions, the author concludes that US GDP per capita will grow at a rate of 0.9% per annum. (2.0 − 0.3 − 0.6 − 0.2 = 0.9). Since the Census Bureau estimates that the US population will grow through 2032 at an annual rate of 0.6 to 0.65 percent, what Gordon is saying is that potential output growth is projected to grow at a rate between 1.5% and 1.55% per year. For the sake of comparison, estimates made by the CBO and by the IMF (Article IV) indicate 2.1% and 2.0%, respectively.

The view from the Fed

Since central bankers normally conduct their policies with an eye on what they perceive the equilibrium real interest rate to be, and given this whole discussion on what probably happened with that rate in recent times, it seems relevant to examine the views emanating from the monetary policymakers in the US.

In May and June of 2014, two members of the Fomc discussed that matter openly. William Dudley, president of the Federal Reserve Bank of New York and vice-chairman of the Federal Open Market Committee (FOMC), made a speech entitled "The Economic Outlook and Implications for Monetary Policy", and Narayna Kocherlakota, president of the Federal Reserve Bank of Minneapolis, talked about "Low Real Interest Rates".

In Dudley's above-mentioned speech the issue involving the level of interest rates in the future was dealt with in just four paragraphs. But the author's ideas were expressed very clearly. "I would expect them to be lower than historical averages for three reasons". (Dudley 2014, p. 5). The first reason was that one could expect greater precautionary saving and less investment for a long time due to the fact that the Great Recession had scarred households and businesses, who had been accustomed to a relatively stable macroeconomic environment. The second reason was that slower growth of the labor force, associated with the aging of the population, and moderate productivity growth would imply a lower potential GDP growth rate, in comparison to the 1990s and the 2000s. Supposedly, the level of real equilibrium interest rates is positively related to the real growth rates of potential GDP. The third reason had to do with recent changes in financial regulation. Higher capital requirements for the banking industry, for example, tend to push down the long-term equilibrium interest rate.

Kocherlakota dedicated his entire speech to the question of low interest rates. And his analysis focused on the "dramatic changes in the demand for and supply of safe assets" observed over the past seven years. In his view, those changes (which might persist over the next five years or so) produced a considerable decline in what he called the mandate-consistent real interest rates. (Kocherlakota, 2014).

The main factors behind that fall would have been tighter credit access, heightened perceptions of macroeconomic risk and increased uncertainty about the federal fiscal policy. First, restrictions to borrow are tighter now than before the crisis, a situation which leads households and businesses to spend less and save more. Those contemplating the purchase of a house, for example, have to acquire more safe assets before going to the market, due to requirements of increased down payments. Second, before the crisis economic agents did not consider a severe macroeconomic shock a relevant contingency. The change in perception increases the demand for safe assets, since they give workers and businesses a sense of protection against macroeconomic risk. The third factor relates to the long-run fiscal problems of the US economy. Uncertainty regarding the nature and magnitude of fiscal adjustments also increases the propensity of individuals to accumulate more safe assets.

On the supply side, the main concern rests on the fact that real estate and asset-backed securities used to be seen as solid financial instruments. But this is no longer true, or at least not as true as in the past. Furthermore, the crisis in the Eurozone showed that papers issued by some governments are not as secure as they were before. Thus, the supply of safe assets has diminished substantially. Caballero and Farhi recall that a study by Barclays concluded that "the world supply of safe assets collapsed from 37% of world GDP in 2007 to about 18% by 2011", a contraction driven primarily by the reassessment of the riskiness of US residential mortgages and sovereign debt in the European periphery. (Caballero and Farhi 2014, p. 111).

The conclusion reached by Kocherlakota was that "for many years to come, the Fomc will have to maintain low real interest rates to achieve its congressionally mandated goals". Thus, the Fomc might have to follow policies capable of producing financial market instability, a risk which needs to be balanced against the risk of deviating from the dual-mandate objectives. (Kocherlakota 2014).

Equilibrium rate is a time-varying concept. In a paper which originally appeared in 2001, two Fed economists (one of them is the current president of the FRB of San Francisco) devised a model which would allow them to estimate the natural rate of interest in the United States. The exercise involved identifying the real rate which over time equated real GDP to its potential. In the early 2000s, that rate fluctuated around 3.0% per annum. Since then, things changed substantially. Graph 3 shows the authors' updated estimates of the natural rate, which became slightly negative since the end of 2012. (Laubach and Williams 2001).

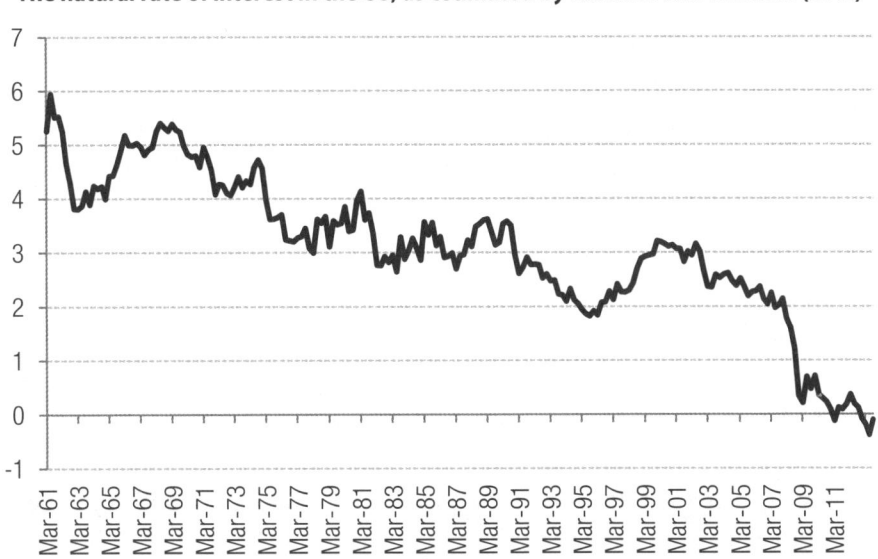

Graph 3
The natural rate of interest in the US, as estimated by Laubach and Williams (in %)

Quarterly data. Latest figure: 2014.II. Source: Thomas Laubach and John Williams, "Measuring the Natural Rate of Interest", Board of Governors of the Federal Reserve System, November 2001. Updated estimates obtained at the FRB of San Francisco.

Members of the Fomc make regular projections of key macroeconomic variables as part of the Fed's communication policy. Let us examine their estimates of GDP growth rates and the target federal funds rate over the longer run.

As to potential growth rates, looking only at central tendency estimates, which exclude the three highest and the three lowest projections, we notice that they started being revised downward in the second quarter of 2011. At that time, the range was 2.5-2.8% per annum. The latest figures, released on September 17, were 2.0-2.3%.

Estimates of the target federal funds rate for the longer run were first published in January 2012. At that time, the average and the median projections were 4.21% and 4.25%, respectively. On September 17, those numbers had fallen to 3.79% and 3.75%, respectively. Recalling that the Fomc sees no change in the long-run inflation rate (2.0% per annum), one can say that what has been revised downward was the real equilibrium rate, in about half of a percentage point.

The behavior of the markets

The fact that part of the debt of the US government takes the form of inflation-protected securities allows us to have an immediate notion of real rates of interest negotiated in the market. Graph 4 shows yields adjusted to constant maturities for 5, 10 and 20 years. Those rates fell constantly from the last quarter of 2008 until the second quarter of 2013, when the Fed gave the first signs of willingness to initiate the tapering of asset purchases. The upward movement lasted for a while, but by the end of 2013 rates had already resumed their downward trend. As shown in the graph, as regards the five-year maturity, rates had been in the negative territory for more than two and a half years. At the time of writing, the real rate was practically zero. As to the 10-year maturity, rates were negative for more than one and a half year and have been slightly positive since mid-2013.

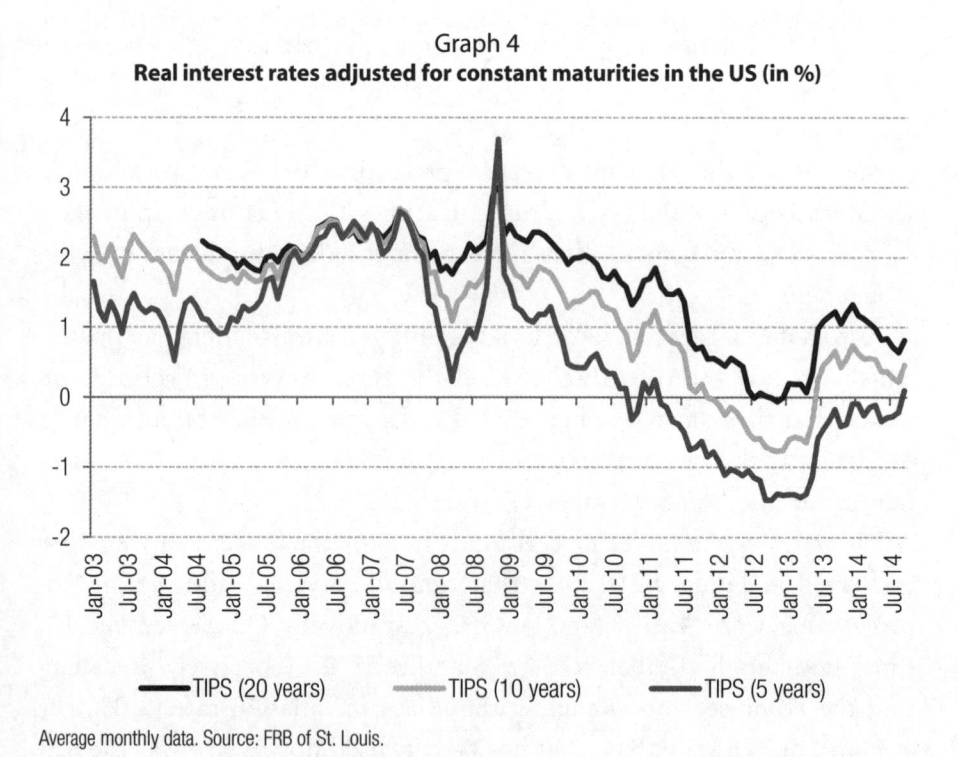

Graph 4
Real interest rates adjusted for constant maturities in the US (in %)

Average monthly data. Source: FRB of St. Louis.

Combining the real rates of interest for different maturities allows us to observe the real forward rates implied by them. If we calculate the five year-five year forward rates for the US, and for the UK and Germany as well, we realize that they have fluctuated significantly in recent times. They all reached very low levels since the beginning of 2011, there being periods of zero or even negative rates. Estimates of the 10 year-10 year forward rates have also been at historically low levels.

Concluding remarks

The story told so far involves facts and some suppositions. Let us try to separate the first from the second ones. And let us consider some alternative suppositions as well.

Facts

- Industrial economies experienced a peculiar behavior in the years prior to the crisis. There was "too easy money, too much borrowing, and too much wealth" (Summers 2013). In spite of this, those economies did not overheat.
- The 2000s saw an increase in financial integration and a lowering of global interest rates. Savings increased in the emerging world, particularly in China.
- Recovery from the crisis has been disappointingly slow. Policy interest rates were brought down to their lower bound. And they are still there.
- Investment rates contracted substantially during and after the crisis, particularly in the Eurozone.
- For the longer run, the Fed has signaled lower rates of economic growth and nominal policy interest rates below the historical level.
- Market interest rates declined further in the post-crisis period. Since 2011, in the US, five-year real interest rates have been negative or close to zero. Five year-five year forward real rates have recently been low in the US, around zero in the UK and negative in Germany.

Suppositions

- There were important structural changes in the industrial world. Demand contracted and the equilibrium interest rate fell. Central banks ran after the declining equilibrium rate. Monetary stimuli produced effects which somehow compensated for the negative impact of the structural changes. Otherwise, growth would have been anemic.
- Equilibrium interest rate has become negative, either before or during the crisis.
- Lack of demand persists in the post-crisis period.
- Output gap is still considerable, in spite of a generalized contraction of potential GDP growth.
- Stagnation or slow growth will prevail for an indefinitely long period. The possible presence of hysteresis effects (long-term damages produced by the extended recession) works in the same direction, by making the economy less productive in the long run. (Ball et.al. 2014).
- Equilibrium real interest rate is probably still negative and will remain so for quite some time. And it shall not return to its historical level.
- Market participants understand and accept the stagnation hypothesis. Their actions reduce real interest rates. Forward rates for relatively distant periods are also affected.

Alternative suppositions

- This whole story of structural problems having caused some sort of a permanent lack of demand is pure nonsense. The presently poor economic situation in the industrial world simply reflects the usual difficulties faced by economies which try to recover from a serious financial crisis. Economic agents are still deleveraging and recovery will take longer than originally presumed. Acceptance of this interpretation, however, would leave without explanation the peculiar events of the pre-crisis period.

- The equilibrium real interest rate might have fallen and it may not return to its normal level. But if it became negative, this is a temporary phenomenon. The problem is more circumstantial than structural.
- Long-term interest rates are not immune to the influence of short-term factors. In the presence of signs of stronger (than expected) economic recovery, medium and long-term rates will adjust accordingly. And this may not take long, at least in the US.
- Rejection of the secular stagnation hypothesis does not rid us from concerns with slow growth in the future. After all, there are good reasons to believe that, due to the working of important supply-side factors like aging population, no major positive shock on productivity gains, etc., potential growth has declined in the industrial world.
- To the extent that slower potential growth implies lower equilibrium real interest rates, chances are that the era of low interest rates on safe assets will persist for a long time.

Concrete possibilities

- The economic scenario in the Eurozone is the least-encouraging one of the industrial world. Since the Fed will certainly start the normalization of monetary policy a lot earlier than the ECB, attention will be concentrated on the Fed's movements.
- The Federal Open Market Committee (Fomc) will surely act in a gradual and careful way, in order to avoid possible negative effects of their actions on the rhythm of economic recovery. But members of the Committee do not hold coincident views. Some of them are clearly more concerned than others about the possible damages caused by aggressive monetary policy accommodation on resource allocation and financial stability.
- Within the Fed, there is a long tradition of respect for the position of the chairman of the organization. In general, the number of formal dissidents on votes of the Committee is kept at low levels.

But dissenting views are expressed through other channels, like public speeches and individual (unidentifiable) votes on the estimated path of relevant macroeconomic variables, especially the target fed funds rate or range.
- Recent signs suggest pressures in the direction of earlier rather than later actions, out of concerns with the formation of bubbles and possible allocative problems created by interest rates being maintained at ultra-low levels for too long.
- Possible premature adjustments to the fed funds rate carry the risk of hurting the recovery process. The dilemma which apparently prevailed in the 2000s, between financial stability and economic growth, may not have disappeared.
- Assuming that when the normalization of US monetary policy begins the economic situation in the Eurozone will still be one of weakness, this fact will maintain a downward pressure on the equilibrium interest rate. This pressure may or may not be compensated by what happens to the savings rate elsewhere in the globe, particularly in China. Through the working of international arbitrage transactions, pressures on the longer segments of the yield curve will be stronger than pressures on the shorter segments.
- The above observation means that the monetary policy transmission mechanism in the US will be affected in a way similar to the one produced by the saving glut of the 2000s, that is, a decline in the steepness of the yield curve. But this will not avoid the strengthening of the US dollar.

References

Archibald, Joanne and Leni Hunter, 2001, "What is the Neutral Real Interest Rate, and How Can We Use it?". Reserve Bank of New Zealand Bulletin, vol. 64, no. 3.

Ball, Laurence, Brad DeLong, and Larry Summers, 2014, "Fiscal Policy and Full Employment", Center on Budget and Policy Priorities, April 2.

Bernanke, Ben S., 2005, "The Global Saving Glut and the U.S. Current Account Deficit". The Federal Reserve Board. The Sandridge Lecture, Virginia Association of Economists, Richmond, Virginia, March 10.

Caballero, Ricardo J. and Emmanuel Farhi, 2014, "On the Role of Safe Asset Shortages in Secular Stagnation". In *Secular Stagnation: Facts, Causes and Cures*, ed. by Coen Teulings and Richard Baldwin, A VoxEU.org Book.

De Grauwe, Paul, 2010, "The Financial Crisis and the Future of the Eurozone". Bruges European Economic Policy Briefings, BEEP, no. 21.

Dudley, William C., 2014, "The Economic Outlook and Implications for Monetary Policy". Remarks before the New York Association for Business Economics, New York, May 20.

Gordon, Robert J., 2000, "Does the 'New Economy' Measure up to the Great Inventions of the Past?". NBER Working Paper 7833, National Bureau of Economic Research, August.

Gordon, Robert J., 2012, "Is U.S. Economic growth Over? Faltering Innovation Confronts The Six headwinds". NBER Working Paper no. 18315, National Bureau of Economic Research, August.

Gordon, Robert J., 2014, "The Demise of U.S. Economic Growth: Restatement, Rebuttal, and Reflections". NBER Working Paper no. 19895, National Bureau of Economic Research, February.

Hansen, Alvin H., [1938] 1939, "Economic Progress and Declining Population Growth". *The American Economic Review*, vol. XXIX, no. 1, part I, March.

International Monetary Fund (IMF), 2014, "Perspectives on Global Real Interest Rates". Chapter 3, World Economic Outlook, April.

Kocherlakota, Narayna, 2014, "Low Real Interest Rates". Speech delivered at the Ninth Annual Finance Conference, Carroll School of Management, Boston College, Boston, June 6.

Krugman, Paul, 2013, "Bubbles, Regulation and Secular Stagnation". The New York Times blog, September 25.

Laubach, Thomas and John C. Williams, 2001, "Measuring the Natural Rate of Interest". Board of Governors of the Federal Reserve System, November.

Solow, Robert, 1987, "We'd Better Watch Out", *New York Times Book Review*, July 12.

Summers, H. Lawrence, 2013, transcript of speech delivered at The IMF Economic Forum, November 8, 2013.

Summers, Lawrence H., 2014a, "U.S. Economic Prospects: Secular Stagnation, Hysteresis, and the Zero Lower Bound", keynote address delivered at the NABE Policy Conference, National Association for Business Economics, February 24.

Summers, Lawrence H., 2014b, "Reflections on the 'New Secular Stagnation Hypothesis'". In *Secular Stagnation: Facts, Causes and Cures*, ed. by Coen Teulings and Richard Baldwin, A VoxEU.org Book.

Part II

Conversations

Affonso Celso Pastore
Laurence Ball
Charles Goodhart
Paul Volcker

5

Conversation with Affonso Celso Pastore

This conversation was held through an exchange of e-mails between J. J. Senna and A. C. Pastore in the first days of March 2013. Professor Pastore was governor of the Central Bank of Brazil between September 1983 and March 1985. He is currently the president of A. C. Pastore e Associados, a consulting firm based in São Paulo.

Inflation targeting

The future of the interest rate policy is largely discussed by government officials outside the Central Bank. The Copom seems not to be pursuing the official target. The behavior of inflationary expectations is rarely mentioned by the Copom members. Do you believe that these and other similar observations justify the concern that the Brazilian Central Bank might be gradually abandoning the inflation targeting regime?

I do not think Brazil will abandon the inflation targeting regime, but there is evidence that the commitment to the target is currently more flexible than in the past. A way to assess the Central Bank's stance is by its reaction curve, which is basically a form of the Taylor Rule. The Bank reacts to two variables: a) the deviations of projected inflation from the target; and b) the deviations of current GDP in relation to its potential (the GDP gap). For a strongly committed central bank to assure convergence of projected inflation to the target (over a given horizon), any time projected inflation reaches one percentage point above the target it will have to raise the basic interest rate by more than one percentage point, meaning raising the real interest rate. Empirical studies published as Working Papers by the Brazilian Central Bank show that until approximately 2007-2008, this conduct (known as the Taylor principle) was obeyed. From 2008 onward, however, this principle has been violated: the interest rate has never responded to the excess of expected inflation in relation to the target, and instead has clearly reacted to the shortfall of actual GDP in relation to its potential.

It's not necessary to consider opinions about the Bank's conduct; it's enough to observe the coefficients of its reaction curve. The intensity of the response of interest rates to a deviation of projected inflation with respect to the target has fallen, and the response has risen substantially to declines in the positive GPD gap (or increases in the negative gap). This is empirical evidence that the Brazilian Central Bank is now less concerned than before with inflation and more concerned with GDP cycles.

For a central bank to be considered properly concerned with inflation, it is not necessary for it to hew to a reaction curve with immutable parameters. This has happened in the United States according to several empirical studies. One was that by Clarida, Gali and Gertler, who show that the Federal Reserve's reaction to inflation was less intense under the leadership of Arthur Burns than under Volker and Greenspan, and it is no accident that the average inflation rates under Burns were higher than those under his two successors. This is an indication that when the commitment to the target weakens, inflation rises, and is clearly in line with the theory of central banking.

Therefore, while the Brazilian Central Bank has not abandoned the targeting regime, it has relaxed its reaction, and the resulting trend will be for persistently higher inflation.

The neutral rate

I suppose that you agree with the idea that the real rate of interest (the policy rate) has been pushed too far, in the downward direction. We all recognize that the so-called neutral level (or neutral range) has fallen considerably. But the Brazilian Central Bank has probably acted too aggressively. Now that the real rate has been set below 2.0% there seems to be great reluctance to

adjust it upwardly. In your opinion, is the weak behavior of economic activity a fair justification for maintaining such a policy?

There can be no doubt that the neutral interest rate has been falling in Brazil. It's enough to look at a graph of the real interest rate (both as indicated by 360-day swaps and the Selic rate deflated by inflation expected 12 months ahead) to verify a strong downward trend. Despite this fact, until recently inflation never showed a tendency to grow. If the market interest rate (the real Selic rate) had been falling faster than the neutral rate, inflation would have had to show a clear rising trend which until recently was declining. Only in the past couple of years have the symptoms of inflationary pressures appeared.

The neutral interest rate is that which balances aggregate supply and demand. In practice, that neutral rate leads to a nil output gap. The constancy of inflation along with the decline of the real interest rate is clear evidence of the continued fall of the neutral rate. But how fast has the neutral rate fallen? Is the entire fall of the neutral real interest rate permanent, or is it partly transitory, meaning a reversion, if only partial, is in store under different circumstances than today's?

To answer these questions it is necessary to examine the concept of the neutral interest rate in more detail. I first present a specification of the IS curve that was common before the 2008-2009 crisis. In this case, the GDP gap was expressed as a function of the real market interest rate in the following form:

$$y_t - y_t^p = a + br_t$$

where y_t is current GDP, y_t^p is potential GDP and r_t is the real market interest rate. The neutral rate is found by setting the GDP gap equal to zero (meaning supply exactly matches demand). This is given by $r^N = -a/b$. An econometric estimate of the IS curve leads to estimates of the two parameters, a and b, that allow extracting an estimate of the neutral rate. I now look to the alternative case, during the 2008-2009 crisis. In this period a form of contagion occurred, so that the strong increase of the (negative) global GDP gap led to an increase in Brazil's negative GPD gap. Indeed, it would be impossible to explain the speed and intensity of the Brazilian recession in that period without counting the contagion from the worldwide recession, which occurred through various transmission channels. In other words, in this period, Brazil's GDP gap depended on the global gap, and the IS curve assumed the form

$$y_t - y_t^p = a + br_t + c(Y_t - Y_t^p)$$

where $(Y_t - Y_t^p)$ is the global gap. If this gap (the world gap) had been zero, the neutral real interest rate would have been the same as in the previous example, but with $(Y_t - Y_t^p) < 0$, Brazil's neutral rate is given by $r^N = -a/b - (c/b)(Y_t - Y_t^p)$, which for $(Y_t - Y_t^p)$ leads to a lower neutral rate than before. In reality, the greater the global output gap, the lower will be the neutral interest rate in Brazil. This simple example leads to two conclusions. First, during the worst phase of the crisis, the neutral interest rate in Brazil fell significantly. Second, it only can remain lower while the contagion from the global crisis continued to affect Brazil. If the global gap were to return to zero, this component determining the neutral rate would disappear. There are no doubts that during the worst part of the crisis, the neutral rate in Brazil fell sharply. But one must consider that this is not a permanent movement, but rather is at least partly transitory.

It's hard to estimate what has happened from that moment (the depth of the crisis) onward, but for sure the depressing effect from the rest of the world is not as strong now as it was in 2009. Various empirical studies have tried to estimate the neutral interest rate in Brazil. One of them was carried out by the IMF, in an econometric work covering several countries besides Brazil. Econometric techniques (such as Kalman filtering) can also be applied to estimate the parameters a and b of the IS curve, as well as what has been happening to the constant term of the reaction curve, which is an alternate way to extract information on the neutral rate's trend. All these studies have concluded that the neutral rate has declined, but also indicate the rate is higher than 2% a year, which is slightly above what is currently happening in Brazil.

But even if the imprecision of these estimates urges caution regarding what the "true" neutral interest rate is, there's another regularity that sheds some light on the subject. For nearly three years the expected inflation rate has stood at around 5.5%, and current inflation has been even higher than this for some time, bordering on 6% a year. This provides indirect evidence that the real market interest rate (and the real Selic rate) is below the neutral level. The reluctance to experiment (by trial and error) where it is can perhaps be explained by the nature of the Central Bank's reaction curve, which these days clearly gives less weight to deviations of inflation from the target than to deviations of actual GDP in relation to potential GDP.

Monetary policy and the exchange rate

The introduction of substantial barriers to foreign capital inflows allowed the government to have some control of the behavior of the nominal exchange rate. To what extent do you think that the heavy hand on the exchange rate market is hurting the conduct of monetary policy?

I first want to mention two pieces of empirical evidence. First, in the presence of price rigidity, there's a strong positive correlation between the nominal exchange rate and the real exchange rate. Second, the evidence about the PPP indicates that a shock in the real exchange rate dissipates very slowly. Although in the long run the real exchange rate only depends on real variables, the conclusion that can be drawn from the above two indications is that it is not only possible to alter the real exchange rate by acting on the nominal rate, this alteration also is highly persistent, and for this reason its effects do not dissipate quickly. Governments that want to produce a weaker real exchange rate in general act by intervening in the foreign exchange market and introducing capital controls, both of which are instruments to guide the real exchange rate.

But this comes with a consequence. The weaker exchange rate raises domestic prices of international goods and heightens inflationary pressures. It's possible to estimate response curves of the consumer price index (IPCA) to an impulse from the exchange rate, and conservative estimates of this pass-through show that in eight months about 6% of the depreciation is incorporated in the IPCA. In May 2012 there was a shift in the exchange rate regime. In the 12 months ending in April 2012, the exchange rate fluctuated (with a good deal of amplitude) around an average of R$1.80/US$. In May there was a depreciation of around 10%, putting the real at about R$ 2.00/US$, where it remained for the rest of the year (again with some fluctuations). The estimate of the pass-through shows that in December the IPCA would have been 0.6 percentage point lower without the depreciation. In other words, without that depreciation, the IPCA would have been 5.2% instead of the observed figure of 5.8%.

There are indications the government would like to continue the depreciation, with the aim of favoring industry. But even if it did so slowly, this would certainly increase the IPCA more, contributing to accentuate the unanchoring of expectations. How does this work?

In an inflation targeting regime, the anchor is expectations, which are affected by the target. If in face of a deviation of expectations in relation to the target, the Central Bank reacts through any of the instruments at its disposal (Selic rate, macroprudential measure), leading expectations (and later inflation itself) to the target, it will keep its creditability high and enhance its capacity to influence expectations. In other words, besides acting through the aggregate demand channel, it also acts though the expectations channel, increasing the efficacy of monetary policy. There is clear empirical evidence that in recent years the expected inflation rate has no longer been influenced by the official central target of 4.5%, but rather by a higher one, currently about 5.5%. So, if a weaker exchange rate raises inflation and the Central Bank fails to react, a new unanchoring will happen, reducing its ability to act through the expectations channel and undermining the efficacy of monetary policy.

This is one of the reasons why the adequate functioning of the targeting regime requires a high fluctuation freedom. Without going into heated and fruitless discussions, it is important to recognize that Brazil has never had a purely floating regime. There have always been heavy interventions, either in the spot market or the future market, as well as frequent actions to control capital inflows. But in the past year there has been a marked shift away from the "dirty float" regime toward what can only be described as a pegged regime with target bands. The country has passed from a situation of forceful interventions to a regime where targets for the exchange rate are increasingly interfering in the efficacy or monetary policy.

Nominal GDP targeting

Finally, you have been following very closely the recent changes in the way monetary policy is conducted in the United States, especially as regards the use of forward guidance mechanisms. As you know, in the academic as well as in the central banking world, there are people who believe that a new monetary policy regime is in order. As a result of discussions along this line, some have proposed the so-called nominal GDP targeting regime. Do you see any merit in such a system? Would it be applicable to a country like Brazil?

The United States is facing a situation never experienced by Brazil. A succession of errors led to a crisis that triggered a "liquidity trap", in which the short-term nominal interest rate has reached zero and cannot fall more. In a case like this, the theory calls for using fiscal policy. But this is not possible due to the excessive public debt. With fiscal measures off the table, the American government has entered an experiment of acting on the long-term interest rate curve, which should stimulate economic activity through various channels. Without this action, the country would be facing deflation and a severe recession. In a scenario like this, it's natural for the main worry to be with GDP, employment and economic activity, particularly because the risk of inflation is nil (the risk is of deflation). Perhaps in this case a regime with nominal GDP targets will work, but this does not apply to Brazil, especially in light of its still-fresh memory of hyperinflation in the late 1980s and early 90s.

6

Conversation with Laurence Ball

The issues covered in this conversation were discussed personally with Professor Ball during his visit to Brazil in the middle of May 2013. He delivered the keynote address at the XV Annual Seminar on Inflation Targeting, sponsored by the Central Bank of Brazil, and paid a two-day visit to the Instituto Brasileiro de Economia (FGV/IBRE), where he made a presentation on the US monetary Policy. The formal conversation was held through an exchange of emails between J.J.Senna and Laurence Ball in the first days of June 2013. Professor Ball teaches at The Johns Hopkins University. He is also a research associate of the National Bureau of Economic Research and a visiting scholar at the International Monetary Fund.

Monetary policy and the employment objective

You have just given the keynote speech of XV Annual Seminar on Inflation Targeting, sponsored by the Central Bank of Brazil. In your address you suggested that monetary policy makers should have an explicit employment objective. It is generally understood, however, that central banks which follow the inflation targeting regime already take into account the estimated output and employment gaps. The example you gave – the ECB – seems to be an exception, derived from the fact that the rules of the game were imposed by the Germans as a precondition for giving up the Deutsche mark. Perhaps the Bank of England would be a more typical example of an inflation-targeting practitioner. In this case, if the economy has been hit by adverse shocks, the central bank avoids forcing the immediate convergence of inflation to target. Frederic Mishkin has called this sort of behavior the "dirty little secret" of central

banking. My question is: doesn't this already give a substantial degree of flexibility to the system? Do we really need an explicit employment objective, as proposed by you at that seminar?

The proposition that it's OK to target inflation without an explicit employment objective depends on the assumption that unemployment always returns to a fixed natural rate. Under that assumption, the worst that the absence of an employment objective can do is magnify short run fluctuations in unemployment. In my view, insufficient attention to employment can have much more harmful effects: because of hysteresis, unemployment may rise permanently, or at least for a very long time, unless policymakers have a clear goal of keeping it low.

The ECB may be an extreme case, but other countries with inflation targets have seen the natural rate of unemployment drift up—in Sweden, for example, the financial crisis and recession of the 1990s seems to have had a permanent effect on unemployment. If Swedish policymakers had a clear employment mandate, they might have followed more expansionary policies and prevented some of the long-term rise in unemployment.

Even if a central bank has an implicit employment objective, this objective is likely to receive less weight than an explicit inflation target. Central bankers are judged more harshly for failing to achieve an explicit target than for failing to achieve an implicit target, because the failure is more clear-cut. The laws governing central banks should make it clear that policymakers will be held accountable for what happens to employment as well as inflation, so that policymakers have an incentive for balanced policies rather than policies that over-emphasize inflation.

The dual mandate

In your defense of an explicit employment objective you seem to have in mind a regime similar to the one practiced in the US, that is, a dual mandate. This type of strategy has not been widely tried. When you propose the dual mandate, do you think of its adoption on a temporary basis, that is, something to last until all the signs of the current crisis disappear, or what you have in mind is something more permanent?

Don't you think that such a model is applicable only to countries where the monetary authorities have already acquired a high degree of credibility? What about economies like Brazil, with a long history and memory of inflation?

Before the 1990s, many central banks said they sought full employment, or some similar goal, as well as price stability. The idea of a single mandate was introduced by Canada and New Zealand, the IT pioneers, in the early 90s. And, in my reading of the historical record, this shift has not been an improvement. It has contributed to long-term increases in unemployment in many countries.

I believe that central banks should restore employment mandates and do so permanently. The problems with a single mandate are not specific to the post-2008 crisis. Even before then, many European countries had persistently high unemployment—often near ten percent—as a consequence of their overemphasis on inflation. Unemployment was relatively low in the U.S. before 2008, and I attribute that largely to the dual mandate.

Certainly it is important for Brazil to avoid a return to extremely high inflation rates. But I do not believe that goal requires a single-minded focus on inflation. The fact that inflation is running near the top of the BCB's target range does not suggest to me that inflation will explode as it did in the 1980s. Again, it is possible for policymakers to be balanced—to put substantial weight on unemployment without being over-expansionary and letting inflation get out of control.

Hysteresis in unemployment

In an article dated March 2009 ("Hysteresis in Unemployment: Old and New Evidence", NBER WP 14818), you gave a specific reason for the suggestion that central banks should not focus too heavily on inflation. The reason is that there is evidence of the existence of hysteresis in unemployment, that is, a given tightening of monetary policy lowers aggregate demand and raises observed unemployment, which, in its turn, through mechanisms still not completely understood, provokes

an increase in the natural rate of unemployment. Your analysis of the experience of the 1980s allowed you to conclude that "there is a significant relationship across countries between the size of the inflation decrease and the change in the NAIRU". And that the change in the NAIRU seemed to be related to the length of time over which disinflation occurred as well. In other words, to reduce high inflation rates costs more than we normally imagine because of lasting impacts on unemployment. Couldn't I then argue in the opposite direction, that is, that central banks should focus heavily on inflation, doing all their best to maintain it low and stable?

It is a fair point that hysteresis makes it costly to reduce inflation, which increases the importance of preventing inflation from rising to a level where disinflation is necessary. However, I believe that many central banks have pursued policies that are more contractionary than necessary to keep inflation low and stable. In the U.S., the Federal Reserve has responded to increases in unemployment by cutting interest rates, and that has pushed unemployment down—and that has happened without inflation taking off. Other central banks--such as the ECB and the central banks of European countries before the euro was introduced—have kept policy tight in the face of rising unemployment. Their inflation outcomes have not been much better than those of the U.S., and their unemployment outcomes have been worse. I'm repeating myself, but I think the key idea is that a policy framework that has a balanced emphasis on both inflation and employment can achieve good outcomes for both variables.

The idea of a 4.0% inflation target

The idea of a 4.0% inflation target was also raised in your presentation at the Central Bank seminar. The motivation would be to lower the probability of reaching the interest-rate zero bound. In a just published paper, "The Case for Four Percent" (Central Bank Review, Central Bank of the Republic of Turkey), you mentioned that one of the objections to this proposal has to do with the impact of high inflation rates on economic growth. You then added that existing empirical works suggest that in order for inflation to hurt growth, it has to be above a given threshold. And that the estimates of this threshold vary considerably, going from 8.0% to 40.0%. Wouldn't the disparities observed in these estimates be a sign that we still do not know much about this issue? This being the case, shouldn't we then be more conservative in choosing the target for inflation?

I would say that a range of estimates from 8% to 40% suggests that 4% is safe—it is only half of the lower bound of the range. In any case, the estimates that you mention, based on cross-country comparisons of inflation and growth, are only one piece of evidence on the costs of inflation. There are also studies that try to measure the specific costs of inflation described in textbooks, such as Stan Fischer's work in the 1980s on relative price variability, and work that seeks to measure the effects of inflation uncertainty on investment. As Paul Krugman has written, the measured costs of inflation from such research are "embarrassingly small."

My intuition about inflation is influenced strongly by the U.S. experience of the 1970s and 80s. The double-digit inflation of the 70s was considered unacceptable by both policymakers and the public, and they applauded Fed Chairman Paul Volcker when he "conquered" inflation in the early 80s. People forget that this conquest meant that inflation was reduced to about 4% in the second half of the 80s. At the time, few people worried that inflation was still too high, and looking back I can't see any significant ways that 4% inflation undermined the efficiency of the economy. The idea that only 2% inflation is acceptable—like the idea of a single mandate—started to become popular only in the 1990s, and I do not think it is supported by history.

7

Conversation with Charles Goodhart

This conversation was held through an exchange of e-mails between J.J. Senna and Professor Goodhart in the final days of March 2014. Charles Goodhart is Emeritus Professor of Banking and Finance with the Financial Markets Group at the London School of Economics, having previously (1987-2005) been its Deputy Director. Until his retirement in 2002, he had been the Norman Sosnow Professor of Banking and Finance at LSE, since 1985. Before then he had worked at the Bank of England for seventeen years as a monetary adviser, becoming a Chief Adviser in 1980. In 1997 he was appointed one of the external members of the Bank of England's new Monetary Policy Committee, a position he held until May 2000.

Free banking

In your 1988 book, *The Evolution of Central Banks*, you showed that the role and functions of central banks evolved naturally and were a necessary part of any modern banking system. However, two of the main writers who had dealt with the subject several decades earlier, namely Bagehot and Vera Smith, although realizing it would be "childish" (Bagehot's word) to think of closing the Bank of England, revealed a theoretical preference for an economy without a central bank. That was the "natural" solution, they thought. In the 1970s and early 1980s, the theme was revived by studies which examined some historical experiences with free banking. The conclusion was that free banking was not as chaotic a system as was generally believed. In 1998, Greenspan somehow endorsed such interpretation. In reference to the US case he said that the system was not "as free as commonly perceived" but also not "nearly as unstable". This view

may have contributed to a sort of a laissez-faire approach of some central bankers. The recent crisis probably changed that in a definitive way. Do you agree with this comment? Among the measures taken after the crisis, both locally and by the international community, which ones would you select as the most promising ones, given the objective of gaining firmer control over the banking industry? What are we still missing in that regard?

Greenspan's adherence to the Efficient Market Hypothesis (EMH) was not widely supported by central bankers outside the US. However, they had a different set of false beliefs. These were:

1. That so long as the monetary authorities maintained stable inflation, there would be no major macro-economic disturbance;
2. That so long as there was no major macro-economic disturbance, the Basel II CARs would guarantee that banks would always maintain sufficient capital to meet difficulties;
3. That so long as banks were Basel II compliant, they would always be seen as strong enough to be able to maintain sufficient wholesale funding to meet any temporary liquidity shortages.

As you know, all these three comfortable myths were proven to be mistaken in 2007/8.

There was another generally accepted error, which was that lending on property, both commercial and residential, was relatively safe, particularly in the USA, where a diversified portfolio of houses, diversified over the whole of the USA, had only shown a small decline in prices once since 1945. People, including the regulators, simply did not see the dangers from credit extension for housing. Possibly the best book on this is by Michael Lewis, *The Big Short*, where what is notable is that the people who foresaw and bet on the basis of the sub-prime crisis were all typically 'loners' who took no notice of the conventional wisdom.

One of the great pities of the regulatory ferment following the Great Financial Crisis (GFC) is that attention has been focused on the banking system rather than on the methods, forms and processes of housing finance. I have myself lived through three financial crises in the UK (1973-75, 1990-92, 2007-09), and all of these have been caused by a bank credit-fuelled housing and property boom. This boom was typically financed by standard retail banks, and the suggestion and claim that somehow the problem was due to nefarious risk-taking in investment or universal banks is, in my view, invalid. It is true that both Bear Stearns and Lehman's were investment banks, but both got into difficulties because of their holdings of mortgage-backed securities, while their derivative books were good, and also because they were not able to access the protection of the Fed.

So I think that much of the direction of regulation since the GFC has been largely misguided, e.g. the Volcker Rules, the Vickers and Liikenen Report. I have attached a paper setting out some of my heretical views on this. ("Narratives of the Great Financial Crisis (GFC): why I am out of step").

Inflation and financial stability

Inflation is a monetary phenomenon and monetary policy cannot affect real variables in a permanent way. Central banks should aim basically at controlling inflation. Over the medium and long run, this is the only task they can be responsible for. Inflation targeting (IT) relies on these principles. Since the recent financial crisis did not affect the validity of these principles, the merits of IT have been kept intact. The crisis made clear, however, that we should care as much about financial stability as we care about macroeconomic stability. And there seems to be a revival of the idea that to achieve two objectives we cannot rely on a smaller number of instruments. In this case, the traditional policy instrument of the IT regime (the interest rate) would continue being managed to achieve macro stability, while macro-prudential instruments would take care of financial stability, aiming at asset prices, credit growth, etc. Speaking generally, since there are many instruments of that sort, do you think they can effectively work within the IT framework? Are we close to understanding how the "separation principle" proposed by Tinbergen can be applicable to monetary policy?

Turning to your queries about macro-prudential instruments, I think that in theory they could work within the inflation targeting framework. Indeed, the general idea currently is that price stability is managed through interest rates adjustments, while financial stability is managed through macro-prudential instruments; and that that should deal with the two objectives, two instruments problem. Of course, macro-pru and monetary policy cannot be fully separated, with many of the instruments of macro-pru, e.g. sectoral capital requirements, impinging on the costs of intermediation, and equally some of the monetary policy instruments, such as QE having an effect on financial stability. Even so, this is no worse that the interaction between fiscal and monetary policies, and should be do-able. But there are other problems with macro-pru; for example, how do you undertake expansionary macro-pru in a depression after a financial crisis, when the micro-prudential authorities will be tightening severely? Also, macro-pru has more direct distributional effects on individual markets, e.g. the housing market, and it may be both politically difficult, and potentially damaging to central bank independence, to take measures which affect some particular financial markets rather than others.

Finally, macro-prudential instruments have not been used much in developed countries until now. With these instruments being untried and their effects uncertain, there is a danger that the monetary authorities may use these initially too timidly to have much effect.

The funding-for-lending scheme

Last year, in an article published by the Financial Times, you showed concern with "the increasing desire of officials to tie monetary policy to real outcomes". That trend was "understandable", but the risk was the abandonment of the hardly-won lessons of the 1970s. A better strategy, you said, involved improving unconventional instruments of monetary policy. The article appeared some six months after the joint initiative of the Bank of England and HM Treasury to launch the funding-for-lending scheme. The banking industry had practically stopped lending to households and firms. The idea then was to stimulate such lending, by assuring funding at below-market rates to banks which effectively increased their loans. You showed sympathy for such program. If we look at the behavior of bank credit since that time, it doesn't seem that it

has been revived. After all, the stock of credit has recently grown at less than 1.0% per annum. Does this mean that that scheme has not been as successful as originally expected? Is the above-mentioned rate of credit growth a poor basis for evaluating the program? Are there lessons to be drawn from this British experiment?

As to your question about Funding for Lending (FLS), I think that it is true that FLS had less effect in encouraging bank lending to the private sector in the UK than some of its proponents, including me, had hoped. But it can always be argued that, without FLS, such lending would have declined much more steeply. Since we can never do the counter-factual of what would have happened in its absence, we can never be absolutely sure that it had less effect than had originally been hoped. Since then, bank lending to the private sector in the UK has begun to expand more rapidly, but in the shape of mortgage lending to persons, largely under the influence of the Help to Buy schemes, but not lending to SMEs; so much so has mortgage lending recovered, that FLS has now been dropped for mortgage lending, and is now only usable for SME lending.

One of the reasons why lending to SMEs has been so slow to recover is that capital requirements on such lending have been increased dramatically, as part of the exercise to raise CARs very sharply since the GFC. With such SME lending being highly risky, and requiring a lot of capital behind it, banks have been unwilling to expand such lending rapidly, except in cases where they are highly confident that they will get repaid and where the spread makes the exercise profitable. Even after the housing crash, mortgage lending in the UK is a better bet for banks than SME lending.

I do not think that policy makers or regulators handled policy, after the immediate crisis in 2008/9 had been defused, very well. I attach a final paper for you setting out my reasons for saying this. ("Why Monetary Policy has been Comparatively Ineffective?").

External member of the MPC

In a not so distant past, decision making in monetary policy used to be in the hands of individuals. The US is an exception, since the Federal Open Market Committee (Fomc) was created in the mid-1930s. Nowadays

decision making by committee is the norm. In the case of the UK, the power to conduct monetary policy was given to a committee – the Monetary Policy Committee (MPC) – at the same time the Bank of England acquired operational autonomy, in May 1997, at the initiative of former Chancellor Gordon Brown. The MPC has an interesting structure. There are five internal officials and four external members. These four members do not have executive functions. As far as I know, such a structure is not found elsewhere. With the benefit of being a former external member of the MPC (1997-2000), how do you evaluate such an arrangement? What other activity can an external member hold while taking part in the Committee? Do you consider this an exportable idea?

There is quite a lot of literature on the optimal size of a committee; in particular Anne Sibert has written on this subject (you could look up the reference if you want to do so). For those central banks where there are a large number of participating members, i.e. the Fomc with the Reserve Bank Presidents, and the ECB with the NSB Governors, there is clearly no room for further (external) members.

In several other countries externals, commonly in the form of economists, either academic or business economists, are co-opted onto the decision-making committee, but in such cases they frequently are also given some degree of internal executive function. Examples are the Bank of Japan and the Riksbank. In other countries where the decision-making is more narrowly held, e.g. Canada and New Zealand, the Governor will frequently assemble meetings, including outsiders, to take advice prior to the Governor's decision.

The Bank of England is only unique therefore in having externals who have no other function. My own experience suggests that this duty only takes up about half of one's time, more than half in the month in which a forecast is being made, and less than half in the non-forecast month. Even so, meetings are frequently arranged, or rearranged, at short notice, which the external really needs to attend, and that makes it very difficult to undertake any other allowable activity, because one is so often having to reschedule. Indeed it would be impossible to do so unless one lived and worked close to the Central Bank.

Because of confidentiality, allowable outside work is really limited to non-commercial activities such as teaching, charitable work or various kinds of administration. I continued to teach at LSE while on the MPC, partly because LSE was so close to the Bank; but Willem Buiter, who was then teaching at Cambridge found that impossible. Since my time, I believe that no other external has continued with part-time academic work, though some have been able to do various work on behalf of government; I think that Kate Barker did her report on the housing market for the Labour Government while still a member of the MPC. Of course externals do undertake, and are sometimes expected to undertake, economic research while serving on the MPC. A good example of that is David Miles' article in the Economic Journal a couple of years ago on the optimal regulatory capital.

There are advantages and disadvantages in having externals without any other executive function in a central bank. It enables the externals to play a much larger role in forecasting, which otherwise would probably fall primarily to the staff. Note that the Bank of England's forecast is the responsibility of the MPC, not of the Bank's staff; whereas in most other central bank committees the forecast is that of the staff, not of the committee. On the other hand it provides an imbalance in the forecasting process between the externals, who can play a larger role, and the internals who are otherwise preoccupied with their executive duties. Furthermore, it does not fully utilise the available time of all external members; though note that no external has ever chosen to depart, because they were not fully used.

8

Conversation with Paul Volcker

This conversation was held through an exchange of emails between J. J. Senna and Mr. Paul Volcker in the middle of August 2014. Paul Volcker was Undersecretary of the Treasury for Monetary Affairs (1969-74), president of the Federal Reserve Bank of New York (1975-79), chairman of the Board of Governors of the Federal Reserve System (1979-87) and chairman of the Board of Trustees of the International Accounting Standards (2000-05). In 2008, he was chosen by President Elect Obama to head the President's Economic Recovery Advisory Board.

In his response to the set of questions which had been sent to him, Mr. Volcker attached a speech he had made in May last year, entitled "Central Banking at a Crossroad". At the occasion, he received the Economic Club of New York Award for Leadership Excellence. He indicated that some of his answers could be found in the mentioned speech. In what follows, the paragraphs in italics are excerpts from that text.

Volcker Rule

In September 2009, in a testimony before the Committee on Banking and Financial Services of the House of Representatives, you suggested that commercial banks, providers of "vital basic services to customers" and which, "taken collectively, are certainly systemically important", should be excluded from risky activities such as proprietary trading and ownership of hedge funds and private equity funds. After all, those institutions have access to central bank support and are potential beneficiaries of taxpayer money. Your suggestion was later defended

by the Administration and became known as the "Volcker Rule". During the debates which preceded the approval of the Dodd-Frank Act, the proposal was substantially watered down, although it apparently maintained some degree of effectiveness.

My questions are: 1) Were you disappointed with the final result? 2) Are there other aspects of the regulatory problem that have not been dealt with by the recent legislation and need to be considered in the future?

Here are some comments in response to your questions. I am also attaching a speech I made last year, parts of which are directly "on point".

Before getting to your questions, let me comment about the Volcker Rule, which you say has been "substantially watered down." I often hear that comment. And, indeed, at almost the last minute of the passage of the law, limitations on sponsorship of hedge and equity funds were eased, but by no means eliminated. I believe the restrictions on proprietary trading are real. I suspect most affected banks will say burdensome and too detailed. No doubt they will also spend millions on legal fees in the search for loopholes. But reportedly many traders have left commercial banks for less restricted pastures. In sum, I am not disappointed except with respect to the complexity. That unfortunately is almost inevitable when the institutions affected make great efforts to circumvent the purposes of the regulation.

More broadly, it is of course true that regulators and supervisors are not exempt from psychological pressures and an inability to foresee the future. They almost inevitably lag behind in analysis and the understanding of the technological forces at work, now more complicated than ever. The particular sources of acute strain – derivatives and sub-prime mortgages in this century, the stock market excesses and margin lending in the 1920's, possibly heavy student borrowing and consumer debt in the next decade – change and are identified too late.

Reform of the financial system should be a continuing process. Only now are steps underway to deal with the problems inherent in money market mutual funds – they are hybrid institutions, part mutual funds, part banks – but not logically regulated as either. They are very large and a channel for amplifying and transmitting market strains.

Meanwhile, little has been done to assure that credit rating agencies (or for that matter auditing firms) are adequately independent and subject to strong professional standards.

Efforts to achieve a common set of international accounting standards have been stymied in part by an inability to reconcile differences with USGAAP.

Even in the area of capital and liquidity standards for banks, there is unfinished business although substantial progress is resulting in greater consensus.

More importantly, the enormous change in the financial world in recent decades – the new technology, the speed of communication, the interdependence, the growth of the "shadow banking system," perhaps most important the change in institutional culture toward trading characterized by impersonal "counter parties" rather than by continuing "relationships." The strong incentives built into present compensation system will require different regulatory and supervisory approaches. The challenge is tough intellectually, politically and practically.

Household-debt crises

Recessions which occur in the wake of financial crises tend to be not only deep but long lasting. Knowing this, policy makers around the developed world took numerous measures to restore the health of the banking system and the confidence of the public and the market on the banks. The sooner the system resumes its normal activities, the faster the economic recovery.
In a recent book (*House of Debt*), Atif Mian and Amir Sufi show that banking crises are usually preceded by household-debt crises and that excessive debt is what explains the size and length of the ensuing recessions. A few other academics had reached similar conclusions. In a conversation with Charles Goodhart held in March 2014[1], he said "I have myself lived through three financial crises in the UK (1973-75,

---

[1] See chapter 7 of this book.

1990-92, 2007-09), and all of these have been caused by a bank credit-fuelled housing and property boom. This boom was typically financed by standard retail banks".

My question is: 1) Is there anything that regulators can do in order to avoid the same sort of problems in the future?

I have been involved in observing and dealing with financial crises even longer than Charles Goodhart – or for that matter longer than Atif Mian and Amir Sufi, whom have written about the seeming inevitability of the speculative excesses that lead to financial stress and breakdown. Hyman Minsky and before him Charles Kindleberger long ago explained how periods of calm and prosperity lead to over-confidence, unsustainable expansion, and then collapse. Regulatory restraints – new or well established – to limit consumer risk, to raise down payment requirements, to expose weaknesses in "repurchase" financing patterns are all inevitably controversial, and sometimes may risk stifling seemingly useful and efficient financing. However, the damage that can result from absence of regulation cannot be dismissed.

Quantitative easing

After the zero lower bound for the basic interest rate was reached in the US, and given the slowness of the economic recovery, the Fed opted to put into practice a program of massive purchases of financial assets. Now, as the economy improves, discussions are centered on the exit strategy. Perhaps a parallel can be made with the Second World War period, when the prevailing understanding was that the Fed should support the Treasury, by acquiring government bonds in the market in such a way as to maintain low the cost of financing to the Treasury. The experiment came to an end only in 1951. Despite concerns regarding the possible costs of the normalization of policy, the Fed managed to successfully eliminate monetary accommodation.

My question is: 1) Do you believe we can expect the same this time?

No doubt, the challenge of orderly withdrawal from today's broader regime of "quantitative easing" is far more complicated. The still growing size and composition of the Fed's balance sheet implies the need for, at the least, an extended period of "disengagement". Moreover, the extraordinary commitment of Federal Reserve resources, alongside other instruments of government intervention, is now dominating the largest sector of our capital markets, that for residential mortgages. Indeed, it is not an exaggeration to note that the Federal Reserve, with assets of three and a half trillion dollars and growing, is, in effect, acting as the world's largest financial intermediator, acquiring long-term obligations and financing short-term, aided and abetted by its unique privilege to create its own liabilities.

Beneficial effects of the actual and potential monetization of public and private debt, the essence of the QE program, appear limited and diminishing over time. The old "pushing on a string" analogy is relevant. The risks of encouraging speculative distortions and the inflationary potential of the current approach plainly deserve attention. All of this has given rise to debate within the Federal Reserve itself. In that debate, I trust sight is not lost of the merits – economically and politically – of an ultimate return to a more orthodox central banking approach.

I do not doubt the ability and understanding of [former] Chairman Bernanke and his colleagues. They have a considerable range of tools and instruments available to them to manage the transition, including the novel approach of paying interest on excess reserves, potentially sterilizing their monetary impact. What is at issue – what is always at issue – is a matter of good judgment, leadership, and institutional backbone. A willingness to act with conviction in the face of predictable political opposition and substantive debate is, as always, a requisite part of a central bank's DNA.

Those are not qualities that can be learned from text books. Abstract economic modeling and the endless regressions of econometricians will be of little help. The new approach of "behavioral" economics itself is recognition of the limitations of mathematical approaches, but that new "science" is in its infancy.

A reading of history may be more relevant. Here and elsewhere, the temptation has been strong to wait and see before acting to remove stimulus and then moving toward restraint. Too often, the result is to be too late, to fail to appreciate growing imbalances and inflationary pressures before they are well ingrained.[2]

Inflation targeting and the dual mandate

Inflation targeting (IT) and the so-called dual mandate, as practiced in the US, are different monetary-policy strategies. In the first case, there is an explicit numerical target for inflation which, if credible, serves the purpose of anchoring expectations. There is a hierarchy of objectives, according to which pursuing the target (over the medium run) is a priority, although the state of the real economy is also taken into account. The second case involves a more balanced approach.

When Ben Bernanke became governor, he apparently attempted to convince his colleagues at the Fed that it would be wise to adopt a new strategy (IT). Alan Greenspan and Donald Kohn, in particular, offered strong resistance. Greenspan defended and practiced what he called the "risk-management" approach, which involves efforts to identify and deal with the main sources of risk to each of the two objectives (maximum employment and price stability). Perhaps for this reason, he was sometimes viewed as hawk, sometimes as dove. Kohn used to stress that the US had benefitted a lot from the full flexibility embodied in the "dual mandate".

My questions are: 1) Do you consider one of these two strategies to be superior to the other? 2) In your opinion, should the US authorities consider the possibility of switching to the IT strategy?

I cover the question of inflation targeting and dual (or triple) mandates for a central bank in my attached speech.

I know that it is fashionable to talk about a "dual mandate" – that policy should be directed toward the two objectives of price stability and full employment. Fashionable or not, I find that mandate both operationally confusing and ultimately illusory: operationally confusing in breeding incessant debate in the Fed and the markets about which way should

---
[2] Paragraphs in italics are excerpts from "Central Banking at a Crossroad".

policy lean month-to-month or quarter-to-quarter with minute inspection of every passing statistic; illusory in the sense it implies a trade-off between economic growth and price stability, a concept that I thought had long ago been refuted not just by Nobel prize winners but by experience.

The Federal Reserve, after all, has only one basic instrument so far as economic management is concerned – managing the supply of money and liquidity. Asked to do too much – for instance to accommodate misguided fiscal policies, to deal with structural imbalances, or to square continuously the hypothetical circles of stability, growth and full employment – it will inevitably fall short. If in the process of trying it loses sight of its basic responsibility for price stability, a matter which is within its range of influence, then those other goals will be beyond reach.

I happen to believe it is neither necessary nor desirable to try to pin down the price stability objective by setting out a single highly specific target or target zone for a particular measure of prices. After all, some fluctuations in prices, even as reflected in broad indices, are part of a well functioning market economy. The point is no single index can fully capture reality, and the natural process of recurrent growth and slowdowns in the economy will usually be reflected in price movements.

With or without a numerical target, broad responsibility for price stability over time does not imply an inability to conduct ordinary counter-cyclical policies. Indeed, in my judgment confidence in the ability and commitment of the Federal Reserve (or any central bank) to maintain price stability over time is precisely what makes it possible to act aggressively in supplying liquidity in recession or when the economy is in a prolonged period of growth well below potential.[3]

In sum, narrowly fixed targets for "inflation," or for "maximum employment" – and an assumption that interest rate or other central bank policy instruments – can and should be set months or even years ahead seem to me ultimately counterproductive. Instead of resulting in credibility, the clear risk in confidence will be undermined, as earlier commitments cannot be met.

---

[3]Paragraphs in italics are excerpts from "Central Banking at a Crossroad".

Neither the state of the economic profession nor practical experience offer grounds for confidence that we can anticipate economic circumstances years ahead.

To be perfectly clear in closing these comments, I do not believe it would be either useful or possible to manipulate the inflation rate in an effort to achieve fixed employment goals.

The ultimate result will be less price stability, and quite likely less employment. Certainly confusion in markets and loss of confidence in the central banks would ensue. I would have thought that lesson has been apparent in Brazil for decades!